SECRETS OF ANGELS, DEMONS, SATAN, AND JINNS

Decoding their Nature through Quran and Science

Mahmood Jawaid

InstantPublisher.com

Secrets of Angels, Demons, Satan, and Jinns

Copyright © 1997, 2001, 2002, 2004, 2005, & 2006 by Mahmood N. A. Jawaid. Portions of this book were copyrighted under the title "The Origin and the Nature of the Jinns – A Scientific Analysis" in 1997, "The Jinns – A Scientific Perspective" in 2001, "Satan – A Scientific Perspective in the Light of the Quran and Science" in 2002, "The Jinns – Revealing the Mystery in the Light of the Quran and Science" in 2004, and "The Angels in the Quran and Science" in 2005.

All rights reserved. No part of this book shall be reproduced, stored in retrieval systems, or transmitted by any means without written permission from Mahmood N. A. Jawaid.

Contact for copies, suggestions, and reporting errors:

mnajawaid@yahoo.com

ISBN: 1-59872-581-5

Printed in the United States of America.

First Print 2006. Reprinted in 2007 after typo correction.

Publisher: InstantPublisher.com

Author's Website: http://mahmoodjawaid.com

Table of Contents

Chapter 1
   Introduction   1

Section I – The Jinns

Chapter 2
   The Origin of the Jinns   5

Chapter 3
   The Physical Characteristics of the Jinns   17

Chapter 4
   The Biological Characteristics of the Jinns   25

Chapter 5
   The Intellectual Ability of the Jinns   33

Chapter 6
   The Spiritual Nature of the Jinns   39

Chapter 7
   The Jinns and the Humans   49

Chapter 8
   Deriving Benefits from the Jinns   57

Chapter 9
   Myths about the Jinns   61

Chapter 10
   Genie in the Bottle – An Analysis   67

Chapter 11
   Summary   69

Table of Contents (continued)

Section II – Satan

Chapter 12
   Who is Satan?   75
Chapter 13
   Satan and the Jinns   77
Chapter 14
   The Psychological Nature of Satan   81
Chapter 15
   The Power and Influence of Satan   87
Chapter 16
   Summary   107

Section III – The Angels

Chapter 17
   The Origin of the Angels   111
Chapter 18
   The Physical Characteristics of the Angels   117
Chapter 19
   The Biological Characteristics of the Angels   127
Chapter 20
   The Intellectual Ability of the Angels   137
Chapter 21
   The Spiritual Nature of the Angels   143
Chapter 22
   The Function of the Angels   145
Chapter 23
   The Famous Angels   169
Chapter 24
   The Angels and the Humans   181
Chapter 25
   Summary   187

Table of Contents (continued)

Section IV – The Demons (Evil Jinns)

Chapter 26
    The Demons   193
Chapter 27
    The Angels, the Demons, Satan, and Demons   203

Appendices

Appendix A
    Satan and Adam[AS]
    –The Sequence of Quranic Events   211
Appendix B
    Electromagnetic Waves   217
Appendix C
    The Origin of the Angels
    – The Other Possibility   223
References   229

Notations

Superscripts:

AS	Alaihis Salaam (peace be on him)
RA	Radhi Allaaho Anho (May God be pleased with him).
SAW	Sul Allaaho Alaihay wa Aalayhee Wasullum (May God have peace and blessing on him and his progeny)
ST	Subhanahoo Ta'ala (Glory be to Him)

English Translations of the Holy Quran:

AA	Translation adapted from "Al-Qur'an," by Ahmed Ali, Princeton University Press, Princeton, New Jersey, 1994.
AYA	Translation adapted from "The Meaning of the Holy Qur'an," by Abdullah Yusuf Ali, Amana Publications, Beltsville, Maryland, 1989.
MHS	Translation adapted from "The Qur'an" by M. H. Shakir," Tahrike Tarsile Qur'an, Inc., Elmhurst, New York, 1990.
MP	Translation adapted from "Holy Quran," by M. Pickthall
TBI	Translation adapted from "The Quran," by T. B. Irving, Amana Books, Brattleboro, Vermont, 1985.

Forward

Praise be to God.

O' God! Shower Your blessings upon Muhammad and his progeny.

Peace be upon you, O Prophet, and the mercy of God and His blessings.

Although the Holy Quran is basically the book of guidance, it also sheds light on scientific subjects such as the creation and the projected end of the Universe, the origin and the development of the human being, human psychology, history, geology, and etc. It is natural for scientific minded Muslims to ponder over the relationship of these verses with the observed scientific phenomena. The section on the Jinns and Satan was the first and the section on the angels is fourth attempt by the author for this approach. In between the two attempts, using this approach he was able to locate how, when, and when Adam[AS] could have appeared and what was their lifestyle and how humanity progressed through the lifetime of the humanity, what technological and social innovations took place at what time.

In the present work the author was able to demonstrate the nature of the angels, the demons, Satan, and the Jinns, their physical and biological characteristics, their intellectual ability, and their interaction with the human being. Most of the English translation of the Quranic verses are adapted from "The Meaning of the Holy Quran" by A. Yusuf Ali. When other translations are used, the initials of the translation or the translator are placed in front of the translation e.g. 32 (27) NQ. These initials are explained under Notation. In some cases instead of citing the verse, its number is cited in the superscript. The statements of Prophet Muhammad[SAW] in the sections titled 'Satan,' 'Angels,' and 'Demons' are cited from "Alim" software, Release No. 4. The Arabic words are usually italicized. Both the Quranic verses and the statements of Prophet Muhammad^{SAW} are given in footnotes. Other references are given under the Reference.

The author is appreciative of Dr. Ken Muschelewicz, Dr. Adana Muscehlwicz, Muhammad Badruzzaman, Sharmina Zaman, Dr. Mohammed Aslam, Dr. Khalid Khan, Amjad Baghdadi, Salmaan Jawaid, Nazihah Malik, Mazahir Shaikh, Fazal Shere, Moniza Hasan, and Dr. Abdul Hameed and Parween Qazi for their support and/or suggestions at various stages in the development of this book. The author is very appreciative of his family members for their support and patience during this work:

> Our Lord! Grant us wives and offspring who will be the comfort of our eyes, and give us (the grace) to lead the righteous. (25:74)

Most of all, the author is highly appreciative of his parents whose efforts have brought him to this stage of life:

> My Lord! Bestow on them Your Mercy even as they cherished me in childhood. (17:24)

To err is human. No effort of a human being, except prophets, can be free form error. Please report any error or suggestion to the author or the publisher. Every effort will be made to correct the error.

Mahmood N. A. Jawaid
Charleston
West Virginia

May 14, 2006
Rabi-ul-Thani 16, 1427

Chapter 1
Introduction

Throughout the history, various kinds of beliefs have existed about spiritual beings. They have been categorized as good, bad or neutral beings with respect to how they affect the human being. They assume various forms in the religions of the world, which include celestial and atmospheric beings, devils, demons, and evil spirits; ghosts, ghouls, and goblins; and nature spirits and fairies.[1]

In Western religions the good spiritual beings are usually called angels and the bad ones are termed demons. In Eastern, ancient, and primitive religions such beings are less categorical. For they may be good in some circumstances and bad in others.[1] Islam classifies spiritual beings into angels (*malaikah*) and the Jinns.[1]

The angels are the chosen creatures and obedient servants of God. They administer the affairs of His Kingdom, and carry out His orders exactly and accurately. They neither do anything on their own, nor do they present any plan of their own.[2] They do not have a free will.

The Jinns, on the other hand, are the hidden being created with a conscience and a free will. They, like human being, inhabit the earth. Their world is parallel to the world of the human being. The existence of an invisible intelligent being living with us on the earth has intrigued the human minds and has prompted many folklore. One of the most famous ones is "The Story of the Fisherman and the Genie" in the famous "Tales of a Thousand and One Nights".[3]

The name Satan is a term of Islamic-Judeo-Christian origin and stands for the Devil. He is a being who is the instigator of all evil acts. The Arabic equivalent of Satan is *al-shaytan*. The first time we are introduced to Satan in the Holy Quran[a] is when he refused to bow to Adam[AS] and challenged

---

[a] Behold! We said to the angels, " Bow down to Adam." They bowed, except Iblees. He was one of the Jinns and he broke the command of

God that he will keep on misguiding the humans. God gave him permission until the end of the world (Appendix A). The proper name of Satan is Iblees.

The term demon is of Western origin and stands for an evil or malevolent spirit. They tempt humans to commit sin and place obstacles for them in developing relationship with God.

Compared to the Holy Bible, the Holy Quran and the statements of Prophet Muhammad^{SAW} shed ample light on the origin and nature of the angels, the Jinns, and Satan. A number of books have been written on the Jinns by past and recent scholars[4-7] in the light of the Holy Quran, the statements of Prophet Muhammad^{SAW}, and the reported experiences of others. We will analyze the Quranic descriptions and the statements of Prophet Muhammad^{SAW} about all three of them in the light of science to understand their origin, their capabilities, and their nature. We will then compare their capabilities and their nature with the human being. Although the term demon is foreign to the Holy Quran, we will make an attempt to explain their nature based on their description in Western religion and matching it with the characteristics of other beings described in the Holy Quran.

---

his Lord --- (18:50)

Then We bade the angels bow down to Adam and they bowed down; not so Iblis. (2:34, 7:11, 15:30-31, 17:61, 18:50, 20:116, 38:73-74)

He refused to be of those who bow down. He was haughty and became one of those who reject Faith. (2:34, 7:11, 15:30-31, 17:61, 20:116, 38:73-74)

Section I

THE JINNS

Secrets of Angels, Demons, Satan, and Jinns

Chapter 2
The Origin of the Jinns

Most of us think that we, human being, are the only being with a free will, conscience, and intellect. The Holy Quran, however, informs us about the existence of another kind of responsible being called the Jinns. They, like the human being, are required to worship only God.[a] The very fact that the Jinns are grouped together with the human being suggests that this worship must be with a free will. It also implies that they choose to worship or not to worship God.

If such a being exists, then where are they and how do they look like? How come we do not come across them? How come science has not discovered them? Since the claim of the existence of the Jinns is made in the Holy Quran, we must turn to it to find the answers to our questions.

The Invisible Being:

Let us first look at the Quranic names for the Jinns. The names used for the Jinns in the Holy Quran are '*al Jinn*'[1], '*al-jaann*'[2], and '*al-jinnah.*'[3] These names are derived from the root word '*janna*', which is the active voice of '*junna*,' '*yujannu*'. The root meaning of '*junna*' and '*yujannu*' is 'to be covered or hidden.' '*Jann*' and '*yajunnu*' are the active voices meaning 'to cover or hide.'[4] The word '*janna*' has been used twice in the Holy Quran to describe the word 'cover'.[b]

---

[a] I have only created Jinns (*al-jinn*) and men (*al-ins*), that they may serve Me. (51:56)

[b] When the night covered (*janna*) him (Abraham) over, he saw a star: He said: "This is my Lord." But when it set he said: "I love not those that set." (6:76)

He knows you well when He brings you out of the earth., and when you are hidden (*ajinnatun*) in your mothers' wombs. (53:32)

The word '*jaann*' has also been used for the stick of Prophet Moses (Moosa[AS]), when it turned into snake.[c] Since we do not understand the miracle of the stick turning into a snake, we cannot really understand why '*jaann*' is used for the snake. We will, therefore, exclude this use of the term from our discussion.

The root of the word suggests that the Jinns are hidden or invisible to the human eye. Their hidden or invisible nature has been identified with reference to Satan,[d] who is one of the Jinns.[e] The Holy Quran suggests that, whereas Satan, a Jinn, and his tribes can see the humans, the human being cannot see them.

Originated from Fire:

The Holy Quran states that the Jinns are made from fire.[f] Satan (Iblees), according to the Holy Quran, felt so strongly about his fiery origin that he refused to bow to Adam[AS].[g] The verses define two qualities of this fire: it is hot wind and is smoke-free.

Explanation in the Light of Science:

The analysis above suggests that the Jinns are made from fire. This fire has the following characteristics:

it is invisible to the human being;

---

[c] And throw down your stick!'. But when he saw it moving as if it were a snake (*jaann*), he turned in flight, (27:10) and (28:31) NQ

[d] --- for he (Satan) and his tribe watch you from a position where you cannot see them --- (7:27)

[e] --- He (Iblees) was one of the Jinns (al-jinn), ---(18:50)

[f] And the Jinn race (*al-jaann*), We had created before, from the fire of a scorching wind (*min naar-is-samoom*). (15:27)

And He created Jinns (*al-jaann*) from fire free of smoke (*mim maarij-im min naar*). (55:15)

[g] --- You created me from fire, and him (Adam) from clay (7:12, 38:76)

it is a scorching wind (hot flame);
it is smoke free.

The fire is usually created by burning wood, coal, gasoline, oil, or natural gas. When the fuel burns, it produces hot gases (Figure 1). The hot gases consist of carbon dioxide and steam and form the flame of the fire. Carbon dioxide is an invisible gas. It is carbon dioxide gas that gives fizz to soft drinks. Hot steam is dry and is also invisible. The steam we see coming out of the boiling water is in reality not steam. It is condensed water mist in the steam.

Most of the fuels have solids and give off carbon particles upon burning (Figure 1). The heat of the flame makes the carbon particle glow. It is this glow that gives the flame its color.[5,6] The same carbon particles form soot upon cooling and make the flame smoky. Thus if we could remove the carbon particles from the flame, the flame would not only be smoke-free, it will also be invisible. The invisible smoke-free flame will, therefore, only consist of carbon dioxide gas and steam (Figure 2).

The Jinns, as described in the Quranic verses, are made from smoke-free flame of fire and are invisible. The smoke-free flame, when described scientifically, will be invisible and free of solids. It will only consist of carbon dioxide gas and steam. Both of these are gases and are invisible to human eye. We can, therefore, infer that the Jinns are made from gases that are the product of fire and are invisible to human eye. We can also infer that it is the gaseous nature of the Jinns that makes them invisible.

The Jinns, as will be explained in the later chapters, can climb up to an altitude of 60 to 70 miles. The lowest temperature within this altitude is well below the freezing temperature of steam.[7] If steam would have been one of the basic constituents of the Jinns, they could not maintain their gaseous nature, since steam would condense (turn into water) and then freeze into ice. We can, therefore, rule out steam as one of the basic constituents of the Jinns. This leaves only carbon dioxide gas as the basic constituent of the Jinns.

Carbon dioxide stays in gaseous form up to an altitude of 70 miles.[8] It cannot be converted into liquid or solid at the temperature and pressure ranges in which the Jinns dwell. We can, therefore, state that, of the two gases that make up the invisible smoke-free flame of fire, only carbon dioxide gas maintains its invisibility in the dwelling region of the Jinns. As such only carbon dioxide gas is the most suitable candidate to be the basic constituent of the Jinns. Since at the time of revelation of the Holy Quran, people were not familiar with carbon dioxide gas, God has used natural, commonly observable, and easily comprehensible phenomena to describe the origin of the Jinns in the Holy Quran.

Supporting Evidence from the Holy Quran:
Other Quranic statements also support the gaseous nature of the Jinns and that they are made from carbon dioxide gas.

<u>Inhabitants of the Earth:</u> We stated that carbon dioxide stays in the gaseous form up to an altitude of 70 miles. It implies that the Jinns, made from carbon dioxide gas will also be confined within this altitude. The Holy Quran suggests that the Jinns are an inhabitant of the earth and its surrounding.[h] It was a group of the Jinns who, while traveling, heard Prophet Muhammad[SAW] reciting the Holy Quran.[i]

---

[h] But we (the Jinns) think that we can by no means frustrate God throughout the earth nor can we frustrate Him by flight. (72:12)

[i] Behold We turned towards you a company of Jinns (quietly) listening to the Qur'an: when they stood in the presence thereof they said "Listen in silence!" When the (reading) was finished they returned to their people to warn (them of their sins). They said "O our people! We have heard a Book revealed after Moses confirming what came before it: it guides (men) to the Truth and to a Straight Path. (46:29-30)

Say: It has been revealed to me that a company of Jinns listened (to the Qur'an). They say `We have really heard a wonderful Recital!. It gives guidance to the Right and we have believed therein: We shall not join (in worship) any (gods) with our Lord. (72:1-2)

Possess Mass: The human being and the Jinns are addressed as *'thaqalan'* in the Holy Quran.[j] The scholars normally translate this term as two worlds and two classes[9,10] referring to the Jinns and the human being. The translation implies that since, being creatures with a free will, they are burdened with responsibility or with sin.[11] The term *'thaqal'*, the singular of *'thaqalan'*, means weight or something weighty.[9] With the exception of this verse, the scholars have always translated the term *'thaqal'* and its different forms in the Quranic verses as weight or its equivalent.[k]

---

[j] Soon shall We settle your affairs, O both you worlds (*thaqalan*)! O you assembly of Jinns (al-jinn) and human being (al-ins) (55:31, 33)

[k] Then shall anyone who has done an atom's weight (*mithqal*) of good, see it. And anyone who has done an atom's weight (*mithqal*) of evil, shall see it. (99:7-8).

God wrongs not even of the weight (*mithqala*) of an atom. (4:40) MP

Nor is hidden from the Lord (so much as) the weight (*mithqala*) of an atom on the earth or in heaven. (10:61)

If there be (no more than) the weight (*mithqala*) of a mustard seed, We will bring it to account. (21:47)

If there be (no more than) the weight (*mithqala*) of a mustard seed and it were (hidden) in a rock, or (anywhere) in the heavens or on the earth, God will bring it forth. (31:16)

Not an atom's weight (*mithqala*), or less than that of greater, escapes Him in the heavens or in the earth, but it is in a clear Record. (34:3) MP

Say: "Call upon other (gods) whom you fancy, besides God. They have no power – not the weight (*mithqala*) of an atom – in the heavens or the earth. (34:22)

And the earth throws up its burden (*thaqal*) (from within). (99:3)
Those whose scale (of good deeds) will be heavy (*thaqolat*), will prosper. (7:8, 23:102)

Then, he whose balance (of good deeds) will be heavy (*thaqolat*), will be in a life of good pleasure and satisfaction. (101:6-7)

Say "The knowledge there of it (the final hour) is with my Lord (alone). None but He can reveal as to when it will occur. Heavy (*thaqolat*) were its burden through the heavens and the earth. Only, all of a sudden will it come to you." (7:187)

When she (pregnant wife) grows heavy (*athqalat*), then both (husband and wife) pray to God their Lord, (saying): "If You give us a goodly child, we vow we shall (ever) be grateful." (7:189)

O you who believe! What is the matter with you, that when you are asked to go forth in the cause of God, you cling heavily (*athaqaltum*) to the earth. (9:38)

Soon shall We send down to you a weighty (*thaqeela*) message. (73:5) As to these, they love the fleeting life, and put away behind them a day (that will be) hard (or heavy) (*thaqeela*) (76:27)

It is He who raises up the clouds, heavy (*al-thiqal*) with (fertilizing rain. (13:12)

It is He who sends the winds like heralds of glad tidings, going before His Mercy, when they have carried the heavy (*thiqala*) laden clouds ---- (7:57)

Go you forth, (whether equipped) lightly (*khifafa*) or heavily (*thiqala*) and strive and struggle, with your goods and your persons in the cause of God. (9:41)

If one heavily laden (*muthqalah*) should call another to (bear) his load, not the least portion of it can be carried (by the other) (35:18)

Is it that you ask for a reward, so they are burdened (*muthqaloon*) with a load of debt? (52:40, 68:46)

They will bear their own burden (*athqalahum*), and (other) burdens (*athqala*) along with their own, ---- (29:13)

They (cattle) carry your heavy (*athqalakum*) loads to lands that you could not (otherwise) reach except with souls distressed. (16:7)

Everything that is made form matter possesses weight. We already know that the human being who is made from cells, which contains about 70 to 80 percent water and 20 to 30 percent solids,[12,13] possess weight. Since the Jinns are made from gases, they will also possess weight, though not as much as humans. The verse is thus addressing two intelligent creatures that are made from things (solid, liquid, or gas) that possess weight. The exception in translation for the Jinns and humans is probably due to not knowing the true nature of the Jinns. Now that we know their true nature there is no need to use this exception. The translation of the verse: "Soon shall We settle your affairs, O both you worlds (*thaqalan*)! (55:31)" would then be "Soon shall We settle your affairs, O both you beings possessing mass."

The Gaseous Molecular Beings:
From a biological point of view, all the life forms are of cellular nature. All the life we know of, for example animals, plants, fungi, protista, and monera, are made up of cells.[l] The cell is their basic building block, which contains about 70 to 80 percent water and 20 to 30 percent solids such as organic compounds and minerals.[12,13] The Holy Quran is telling us that there is another kind of life which the science has yet to discover. It is of gaseous and molecular nature. Its basic building block is gaseous molecules namely carbon dioxide (the individual particles of a gas are called atoms or molecules). The statement of Prophet Muhammad[SAW] suggests that, just as there is a host of cellular beings of increasing complexity, there could be a host of molecular beings of increasing complexity.[m]

---

[l] We created human being from sounding clay, from mud molded into shape and the Jinn race, We had created before, from the fire of a scorching wind. (15:26-27)

He created human being from sounding clay like unto pottery. And He created Jinns from fire free of smoke. (55:14-15)

You (God) created me (Satan) from fire, and him (Adam) from clay. (7:12, 38:76)
[m] They (the Jinn) asked him (Prophet Muhammad) about their
provision and he said: Every bone on which the name of God is recited

Whereas the human being is the most complex cellular being, the Jinns could be the most complex molecular being. Whereas the human being, from among the cellular being, is given free will and is made responsible for his actions, the Jinns, from among molecular beings, are given free will and are made responsible for their actions.

The concept that molecules could have life may sound strange to the students of science, but it should not be surprising to the students of the Holy Quran. All the things, according to the Holy Quran, have been given guidance.[n] It is because of this guidance that everything in the universe (heavens and the earth), according to the Holy Quran, glorifies God.[o]

A thing can only glorify God if it knows that it exists and has the knowledge that it has been created by God. A thing that knows that it exists must be conscious of its existence and that is what life is all about. Hence from Quranic point of view, every atom and molecule in the universe has life of its own. The

---

is your provision. The time it will fall in your hand it would be covered with flesh, and the dung of (the camels) is fodder for your animals. Prophet Muhammad [SAW] said: Don't perform istinja (cleaning private parts after relieving) with these (things) for these are the food of your brothers (Jinn). (Sahih Muslim)[14]

[n] He (Moosa) said (to Firon): "Our Lord is He who gave to each (created) thing its form and nature, and further gave (it) guidance." (20:50)

[o] The seven heavens and the earth, and all beings therein, declare His glory. There is not a thing but celebrates His praise and yet you understand not how they declare His Glory! (17:44)

See you not that it is God whose praises all beings in the heavens and on the earth do celebrate ---- Each one knows its own (mode of) prayer (*salah*) and praise (*tasbeeh*). (24:41)

Whatever is in the heavens and on the earth does declare the Praises and Glory (*yosabbiho*) of God. (59:24, 62:1, 64:1)

Whatever is in the heavens and on the earth, let it declare the Praises and Glory (*sabbaha*) of God. (57:1, 59:1, 61:1)

Holy Quran has also given us glimpses of their feelings.ᵖ These glimpses suggest that:

> the sun, the moon, the stars, the hills, the trees, and the animals worship God;
> thunder, angels, birds, and hills celebrate praise of God;

ᵖ See you not that to God bow down in worship all things that are in the heavens and on the earth - the sun, the moon, the stars, the hills, the trees, the animals, and a great number among mankind? (22:18)

See you not that it is God whose praises all beings in the heavens and the earth do celebrate, and the birds (of the air) with wings outspread? Each one knows its own (mode of) prayer and praise. And God knows well all that they do. (24:42)

They became like a rock and even worse in hardness. For among rocks there are some from which rivers gush forth; others there are which when split asunder send forth water; and others which sink for fear of God. (2:74)

Had We sent down this Quran on a mountain, verily you would have seen it humble itself and cleave asunder for fear of God – (59:21)

We indeed offer the Trust to the heavens, and the earth, and the mountains; but they refused to undertake it, being afraid thereof; but man undertook it - He was indeed unjust and foolish. (33:72)

Thunder repeats His praises, and so do the angels, with awe (13:13)

We bestowed Grace aforetime on David (Dawood) from Ourselves: "O you Mountains! Sing you back the Praises of God with him! And you birds (also) --" (34:10)

It was We that made the hills declare, in unison with him (David (Dawood)), Our Praises, at eventide and at break of day, and the birds gathered (in assemblies); all with him did turn (to God). (38:18-19)

It was our power that made the hills and the birds celebrate Our praises with David (Dawood). (21:79)

rocks (stones) and mountains crack open because of the fear (*khashiyah*) of God;

the heavens, the earth, and the mountains, realizing that the Trust was too heavy of a burden, refused to accept it.

We cannot perceive life in inanimate objects, but that is a limitation of our intellect and senses.

It should be noted that just as every cell is not a human being, every carbon dioxide molecule could not be a Jinn. Just as human being is the soul residing in a special arrangement of cells, the Jinns could be the soul residing in a special arrangement of carbon dioxide molecules. The Holy Quran suggests that the term soul (*nafs*) is applicable to both the human being and the Jinns.[q]

Summary:
The life form we are familiar with is of cellular origin. This includes animals, plants, fungi, protista, and monera. The cell is their basic building block, which contains about 70 to 80 percent water and 20 to 30 percent solids such as organic compounds and minerals. The human being is the most complex and most intelligent being of this life form. The Holy Quran informs us about the existence of another class of intelligent being on this earth called the Jinns who are made from fire. A scientific analysis of fire, how it is created, what comes out of it, and the Quranic description of the creation of the Jinns, suggests that the Jinns are made from gases (carbon dioxide and water vapor) that are produced from the fire. The Jinns are, probably, made from carbon dioxide gases. The gaseous origin of the Jinns implies that the basic building block of the Jinns (molecule) is about 5,000 to 50,000 smaller than the basic building block of the human being (cell). Assuming that the mass of both the Jinns and the human being is proportional to the mass of their basic building block, the mass of the human being will be 10 to 10,000

---

[q] If We had so willed, We could certainly have brought every soul (*nafs*) its true guidance: But the Word from Me will come true, "I will fill Hell with Jinns (*al-jinnah*) and men (*al-naas*) all together. (32:13)

trillion times more than the Jinns. The statements of Prophet Muhammad^{SAW} suggest that there could be a host of living molecular gaseous beings made from gaseous molecules. The Jinns are probably the most complex and most intelligent being of molecular gaseous life form. Whereas the human being, from among the cellular beings, is given free will and is made responsible for his actions, the Jinns, from among the molecular beings, are given free will and are made responsible for their actions.

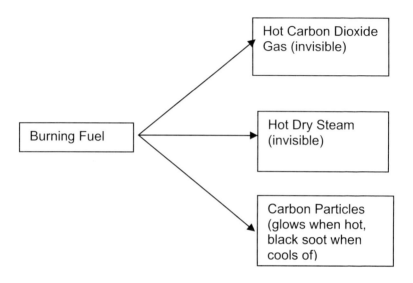

Figure 1: The Components of a Burning Fuel.

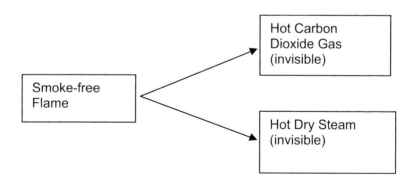

Figure 2: The Components of a Smoke-free Flame.

Chapter 3
The Physical Characteristics of the Jinns

The physical characteristics of a substance depend upon the physical characteristics of the basic building block of that substance. For example, the physical characteristics of a block of iron are determined by the physical characteristics of iron particles. Logic suggests that the physical characteristics of the Jinns, being made of gases, will be dictated by the physical characteristics of gases, especially carbon dioxide molecules.

Weight:
We have already made a case that, since the Jinns are made from carbon dioxide gas, they will possess mass. Since carbon dioxide is lighter than cell, the mass of the Jinns could be 10 to 10,000 trillion times lighter than that of the humans.

Visibility and Perceptibility:
Compared to solid and liquid particles, gas particles are furthest apart from each other. A space that contains 24,000 particles (molecules) of iron or 9,400 particles (molecules) of water will only contain six particles (molecules) of air.[1,2] The individual molecule of any substance is invisible. But with so many molecules of iron and water jammed together, they become visible and touchable. In case of gases, presence of only few molecules in a large space not only makes them invisible, even their presence cannot be sensed. The presence of the Jinns, therefore, cannot be sensed either by sight or touch.

Speed:
The carbon dioxide molecules move at an average speed of about 850 miles per hour.[3] The average speed of the Jinns, a being made from gaseous molecules, should be the same.

According to the Holy Quran, a powerful Jinn sitting in the court of Prophet Solomon (Sulaiman[AS]) claimed that he could bring the throne of the Queen of Saba before the closing of the court.[a] Prophet Solomon (Sulaiman[AS]) held his court in Jerusalem, while the throne of the Queen of Saba was in the city of Saba, which was near Sana in Yemen. Approximate distance between the two cities is about 1,500 miles. Assuming that the court proceeding lasted for three to four hours, the calculated speed of this Jinn, based on a round trip distance of 3,000 miles, would be close to the predicted speed. It would have taken a human being about six days, traveling twelve hours a day on a horse at a speed of forty miles per hour, to travel the same distance in those days.

Space Adventure:
Compared to solids and liquids, gases are less dense. A cubic feet of air will weigh only an ounce[2], whereas a cubic feet each of iron and water will weigh 492 pounds and 62 pounds, respectively[2]. The dense nature of solids and liquids keeps them close to the earth's surface due to strong gravitational force. The light nature of gases allows them to spread up to an altitude of about 400 miles due to weak gravitational force. This space forms the atmosphere[4] of the earth (Table 1) and contains oxygen, nitrogen, and carbon dioxide gases, water vapors, and dust. Three quarters of the air mass in the atmosphere lies beneath 35,000 feet (7 miles). The air gets thinner higher up. Beyond 300 miles from the earth's surface there is hardly any air.[4] The Jinns, a being made from gases, will be limited to this altitude. They will also be limited to this altitude due to their velocity. It requires a velocity of 25,000 miles per hour for a body of mass to break free from the earth's gravity.[5] Since the speed of Jinns is only around 850 miles per hour, they do not have the power to escape the earth's atmosphere.

According to the Holy Quran, the altitude the evil Jinns can fathom is further constrained by shooting stars, which beautify the lowest heaven and guard against the evil spirits

---

[a] Said an Ifrit (a large, powerful jinn, reputed to be wicked and crafty), of the Jinns (al-jinn): "I will bring it (the throne of the Queen of Saba) to you before you rise from your council: indeed I have full strength for the purpose, and may be trusted." (27:39)

(*shayateen*) by driving them away.[b] The term *shayateen* refers to the evil Jinns. The terms *kawaakib* (plural of *kaukab*) and *masaabeeh* (plural of *misbaah*) in the Quranic verses stand for all the luminary objects in the sky, which by definition include stars, planets, comets, and shooting stars (*shihaab, shohoba*). These luminary objects are dispersed in the lowest and the nearest of the seven heavens. The lowest heaven is also the first heaven of the earth we reside in. The rest of the heavens are surrounding the first heaven, and are one on top of another.[c] The terms flaming fire[72(8)], bright flaming fire[15(18)], flaming fire of piercing brightness[37(10)], and missiles[67(15)] refer to the shooting stars.

The shooting stars, also known as meteors, are the streak of light that results from the entry of a small interplanetary solid particle into the earth's atmosphere. The streak of light appears at an altitude of 60 to 70 miles and disappears around an altitude of 50 to 60 miles. The earth's atmosphere is surrounded by these interplanetary solid particles. Every day the earth's atmosphere

---

[b] It is We (God) who have set out the Zodiacal Signs (*brooj*) in the heavens, and made them fair-seeming to (all) beholders; And (moreover) We have guarded them from every evil spirit accursed; But any that gains a bearing by stealth is pursued by a flaming fire, bright (to see). (15:16-18)

We (God) have indeed decked the lower heaven with beauty (in) the stars (*kawaakib*), -- (for beauty) and for guard against all obstinate rebellious evil spirits, So they should not strain their ears in the direction of the Exalted Assembly but be cast away from every side, Repulsed, for they are under a perpetual penalty, Except such as snatch away something by stealth, and they are pursued by a flaming Fire, of piercing brightness. (37:6-10)

And We have, (from of old), adorned the lowest heaven (*as-samaa-ud-dunya*) with lamps (*masabeeha*), and We have made such (Lamps) as missiles to drive away the Evil Ones (*shyateen*), and have prepared for them the penalty of the Blazing Fire. (67:5)

[c] And (have We not) built over you the seven heavens. (78:12)
He (God) who created the heavens one above another (*tibaqaa*) ---- (67:3)

encounters about one million solid particles that are brighter than stars and about two hundred million solid particles that are bright enough to be visible by naked eye. These particles enter the earth's upper atmosphere (around an altitude of 60 to 70 miles) at a very high speed (20 to 40 miles per second) and collide with gas particles. The collision causes the solid and gas particles to become luminous. As these particles penetrate lower in the atmosphere they start to crumble and fragment. Sometimes these particles breakdown producing one or more luminous bursts followed by a bright terminal burst at the end of the visible path.[6]

The Quranic verses cited above suggest that the shooting stars drive away the Jinns from snatching or prying into the secrets of heaven. The meteoritic activity starts around an altitude of 60-70 miles and ends around an altitude of 50 to 60 miles. It can therefore be inferred that the Jinns are restricted within an altitude of 60 to 70 miles. The verses suggest that it is only the bad Jinns (*shayateen*) who try to cross this altitude and are driven back to the earth by meteorites. It can also be inferred that the good Jinns stay well below this altitude. Perhaps the good Jinns know that climbing higher in space to intercept heavenly communication is an unacceptable act for them and they must stay below this altitude.

The Quranic verse suggests that the Jinns, before the revelation of the Holy Quran, had the ability to climb higher than the zone of meteoritic activity (60 to 70 miles).[d] Probably during the revelation of the Holy Quran, their access to higher level was blocked by the shooting stars. It is probable that a significant increase in meteoritic activity coincided with the revelation of the Holy Quran. Since the meteors are fragments of comets, one or more comets may have passed through the earth's atmosphere just before the revelation of the Holy Quran.

---

[d] And we pried into the secrets of heaven (*as-samaa-a*); but we found it filled with stern guards and flaming fires (*shohoba*). `We used indeed to sit there in (hidden) stations to (steal) a hearing; but any who listens now will find a flaming fire (*shihaab*) watching him in ambush. `And we understand not whether ill is intended to those on the earth or whether their Lord (really) intends to guide them to right conduct. (72:8-10)

Compared to air, carbon dioxide gas is fifty two percent heavier. Since the Jinns are made from carbon dioxide, they should stay close to the surface of the earth. However, we just explained that they could fly up to an altitude of 60 to 70 miles. It will only be possible if they can gallop or inhale a bunch of air. This will make them lighter and lift them up in the sky. When they want to come down, all they need to do is exhale the air they had inhaled earlier to go up.

Penetrative Ability (Permeability):
The gas molecules are highly penetrable. These molecules can penetrate into minute pores without even being perceptible. Most of the empty spaces in and around the earth are actually filled with air that is a mixture of gases. The gases not only fill empty space, liquids can also absorb them. The Jinns, being made from gases, will be highly penetrable. They will be able to penetrate into pores of solids and be absorbed by liquids. They will, however, be contained within the earth's atmosphere due to gravitational force of the earth. They will be able to do all of this without ever being perceptible.

Since oxygen is absorbed in our blood through lungs, the Jinns, being made from gaseous molecules, could have the ability to enter the blood stream through lungs. From there, they could penetrate anywhere in the human body. The statements of Prophet Muhammad[SAW] seems to support this inference.[e]

---

[e] Verily Satan circulates in the body like blood. (Sahih Muslim)[7]

Satan penetrates in man like the penetration of blood (in every part of body). (Sahih Muslim)[8]

Verily Satan flows in the blood stream of Adam's descendent. (Sunan Abu Dawood)[9]

Verily Satan influences arteries and veins through blood. (Sahih Bukhari and Sahih Muslim)[10]

Size and Shape:

Gases exhibit great expansion and contraction capability with changes in temperature and pressure.[11] A two-fold increase in pressure will reduce the gas volume by half. A two-fold increase in temperature will cause a two-fold increase in its pressure or volume. This characteristic of gas will allow the Jinns to have flexible size and shape and will allow them to adopt any size or shape. The volume and shape of solid substances does not change to that extent under such circumstances.

Power:

High-pressure gases generate power and work upon expanding. Steam and gas turbines, internal combustion engine, jet engine, and rocket engines employ this characteristic of gas to generate electricity and to operate machinery, automobiles, trains, aircraft, and rockets.[12] This characteristic of gas will allow the Jinns to generate power. During the Prophethood of Prophet Solomon (Sulaiman^{AS}), the Jinns worked as builders and divers for him. They made arches, images, basins, and cauldrons.[f]

Transformation into Animal Forms:

The Jinns seem to have the ability to transform themselves into human and animal form. In the battle of Badr during the time of Prophet Muhammad^{SAW}, Satan appeared in the form of Suraaqah ibn Malik, the leader of the tribe of Banu Bakr, and encouraged Quraish to fight against Muslims.[13,14] He also went to Badr with a battalion of young fighters, but ran away when he saw the angels on the side of Muslims.

We mentioned earlier that the Jinns probably inhale air to rise up in the sky. What if they also have the ability to inhale

---

[f] Then We subjected the Winds (*al-reeh*) to his (Sulaiman) power, to flow gently to his order, withersoever he willed - As also the evil (*al-shayaateen*), (including) every kind of builder and diver - As also others bound together in fetters. (38:36-38)

They worked for him as he desired, (making) Arches, Images, Basins, as large as Reservoirs, and (cooking) Cauldrons fixed (in their places): "Work you, Sons of David, with thanks! But few of My servants are grateful. (34:13)

and exhale liquids and solids. Since they have the flexibility in size and shape due to their gaseous nature, they should be able to acquire any shape and size, including human and animal forms. This may explain their transformation into animal or human form. They can revert back to their original form by exhaling the solids and liquids.

Summary:
The gaseous nature of the Jinns makes them highly imperceptible and penetrable. It gives them great power and flexibility in size and shape. They can also travel at an average speed of about 850 miles per hour, and can fathom the space up to an altitude of 60 to 70 miles. They probably have the ability to inhale and exhale solid, liquid, and gas. By inhaling and exhaling air, they should be able to go up and down in altitude, respectively. By inhaling solids and liquids and having flexibility in size and shape, they should be able to acquire human and animal forms.

TABLE 1

The Earth's Atmosphere[4]

Name of the Earth's Layer	Distance Range from the Earth's Surface	Condition
Troposphere	0 to 7 miles	Contains three quarter (75%) of air in the atmosphere. Most of the weather activity occurs in this layer.
Stratosphere	7 to 30 miles	It is a calm region. Aircrafts fly in this layer.
Mesosphere	30 to 50 miles	If meteors fall in this layer, they burn up, causing shooting star.
Thermosphere	50 to 300 miles	It contains the electrically charged particles from which radio waves can be bounced around the world.
Exosphere	more than 300 miles	This is the final layer before the outer space. It hardly contains any air. There is no definite upper limit to this layer.

Chapter 4
The Biological Characteristics of the Jinns

Life as we know it exhibits certain characteristics. For example, it has a limited life span, it procreates, consumes food, and do purposeful work.[1] In this chapter we will explore if the Jinns exhibit some of these characteristics.

Death:
The Holy Quran states that many generations of Jinns have already passed away.[a] Thus just like humans and other living organism, the Jinns, after their birth, spend their life on this planet and then die.

The Holy Quran states that every soul has to suffer death.[b] The term soul (*nafs*) is applicable to both the human being and the Jinns.[c] The Holy Quran is thus suggesting that, like humans, the Jinns must also suffer death. Satan, a Jinn, knew that one day he will die. He, therefore, specifically asked God to grant him life until the end of the world.[d]

Life Span:
The above section implies that the Jinns have a limited life span. The Holy Quran or Prophet Muhammad[SAW] do not mention their

---

[a] Such are they against whom is proved the Sentences among the previous generations of Jinns (al-jinn) and men (al-ins), that have passed away; for they will be (utterly) lost. (46:18, 41:25)

[b] Every soul (*nafs*) shall have a taste of death. ---(3:185, 21:35, 29:57)

[c] If We had so willed, We could certainly have brought every soul (*nafs*) its true guidance: But the Word from Me will come true, "I will fill Hell with Jinns (*al-jinnah*) and men (*al-naas*) all together. (32:13)

[d] He said: "Give me respite till the day they are raised up." (God) said: "Be you amongst those who have respite." (7:14-15)

life span. According to some other sources, their life span is in hundreds of years, almost ten times that of the humans.

Procreation:
Procreation is the most extraordinary attribute of living organisms. It is necessary because the individual members of species have limited life span. If the Jinns self-replicate, they should have children. The Holy Quran states that Satan (Iblees) has children and tribes.[e] Since Satan belongs to the class of the Jinns, it can be inferred that the Jinns in general have progeny and tribes. As mentioned earlier, the Holy Quran also states that many generations of Jinns have already passed[46:18, 41:25]. The generations can only be a result of self-replication.

Gender:
According to the Holy Quran most of the things, especially the living organisms, exist in pairs.[f] Most of the animals exist in pairs as male and female for the purpose of self-replication. The Holy Quran specifically mentions masculine Jinns.[g] If there are masculine Jinns, there must also be feminine Jinns. It can, therefore, be stipulated that the Jinns also exist in pairs, male and female.

---

[e] Will you then take him (Satan) and his progeny (*dhurriat*) as protectors rather than Me? (18:50)

He (Satan) and his tribes watch you from a position where you cannot see them. (7:27)

[f] Glory to God, who created in pairs all things that the earth produces, as well as their own (human) kind and (other) things of which they have no knowledge. (36:36)

That has created pairs in all the things. (43:12)

And of everything We have created pairs. (51:49)

[g] True there were men (*rijaal*) among mankind who took shelter with the masculine (*rijaal*) among the jinns, but they increased them in sin and disbelief. (72:6) (N.Q.)

Food Consumption:

The life we know from the scientific perspective is of cellular origin. The basic unit of this life is cell. Some living organisms only consist of one cell. Most of the living organisms, however, are multicellular. The human body is composed of billions of cells. The primary food source of all the animals is plant, which is also of cellular nature. Whereas, herbivorous animals only consume plant as food, carnivorous animals consume animal as food. Humans consume both plants and animals as food. Since humans and animals, which are of cellular origin, consume food composed of cells, logic suggests that the Jinns who are made from carbon dioxide gas will consume carbon dioxide gas as food.

    Food serves two purposes. It maintains the animal body by replacing worn out cells, and provides energy for the animals to do purposeful work. Since the Jinns also have limited life span, they should also need food for both maintenance purpose and to do purposeful work.

    The Holy Quran does not mention if the Jinns consume food. However, the following statements of Prophet Muhammad^{SAW} suggest that bones covered with flesh, animal dung, and coal is the source of their food.[h] The decay of flesh left

---

[h] The Prophet^{SAW} said: "They (bones and the animal dung) are the food of the Jinns. The delegate of Jinns of (the city of) Naseebeen came to me --- how nice those Jinns were --- and asked me for the remains of human food. I invoked God for them that they would never pass by a bone or animal dung but find food on them." (Sahih Bukhari)[2]

When a group of the Jinns visited the Prophet^{SAW} they requested him: Tell your people (*ummat*) not to use bones or animal dung or coal for cleaning their private parts, because God has made these a provision for them." So the Prophet^{SAW} forbade us from those items. (Sunan Abu Dawood)[3]

They (the Jinn) asked him (Prophet Muhammad) about their provision and he said: Every bone on which the name of God is recited is your provision. The time it will fall in your hand it would be covered with flesh, and the dung of (the camels) is fodder for your animals. The Messenger of God^{SAW} said: Don't perform istinja (cleaning private parts

on bones and animal dung by bacteria generates carbon dioxide and other gases. The coal also produces gases upon burning. The Jinns probably consume carbon dioxide gases generated by the decay of flesh, dung, and burning of coal.

Purposeful Work:
The living organism can also carry out other forms of purposeful work, such as the mechanical work of locomotion. It has already been stated in the previous chapter that, during the Prophethood of Prophet Solomon (Sulaiman^{AS}), the Jinns worked as builders and divers for him. They made arches, images, basins, and cauldrons.$^{34\ (13),\ 38\ (36\text{-}38)}$

Highly Complex Gaseous Being:
The structure of cellular living organisms is complicated and highly organized. They are composed of cells, which possess intricate internal structures containing many kinds of complex molecules. As mentioned in Chapter 1, the statement of Prophet Muhammad^{SAW} suggests the existence of animals for the Jinns.[4] Just as humans have animals of cellular origin for their consumption and benefit, the Jinns may have gaseous animals for their consumption and benefit. These animals must be of their own kind (made of gaseous molecules). Logic suggests that if there are multiple species of gaseous origin they must vary in complexity. Although varying complexity in cellular organisms implies some sort of structure, it may not hold true among the gaseous (molecular) beings. Had it been so, we should have noticed some sort of organization in gases.

Just as humans are the most complex species among living organisms of cellular origin, the Jinns could be the most complex species among living organisms of gaseous origin.

Time of Appearance:
The Holy Quran states that the Jinn race was created before the human being.^{i} When God created Adam^{AS} and presented him

---

after relieving) with these (things) for these are the food of your brothers (Jinn). (Sahih Muslim)[4]

^{i} And the Jinn race (*Al-Jaann*), We had created before, from the fire of a scorching wind. (15:27)

before the angels, Satan (Iblees), one of the Jinn, was already in existence.[j] He had probably even watched the different stages Adam[AS] went through during his creation.[k] A statement of Prophet Muhammad[SAW] also suggests that the Jinns were created before the human being.[5]

When Adam[AS], the first human being, set foot on the earth, the support system needed for his survival must have been in place before his appearance. This would at a minimum include air to breathe, water to drink, and plants and animals to eat. The same must be true for animals and plants. Thus water, carbon dioxide, sunlight, and minerals must have been present before plants came into existence. Obviously, carbon dioxide, the basic constituent of the Jinns, must have been present much before the appearance of the human being.

Scientists speculate that the earth came into existence about 4,800 million years ago. The primitive atmosphere consisted of hydrogen, ammonia, methane, and water. Hydrogen was soon lost and methane and ammonia converted into nitrogen, carbon monoxide and carbon dioxide. Since carbon dioxide, the basic constituent of the Jinns, is speculated to have been present since almost the birth of the earth (4,800 million years ago), it is reasonable to assume that the Jinns came into existence soon after the creation of the earth. The Homo erectus (from whom the human being evolved) originated only about two million years ago.[6-8]

---

[j] Behold, your Lord said to the angels: " I am about to create man from clay. When I have fashioned him (in due proportion) and breathed into him My spirit, fall you down in obeisance unto him." So the angels prostrated themselves, all of them together. Not so Iblees. He was haughty, and he became one of those who reject Faith. (38:71-74)

[k] (God) said: "O Iblees! what is your reason for not being among those who prostrated themselves?" (Iblees) said: " I am not one to prostrate myself to man, whom You created from sounding clay, from mud molded into shape. (15:32-33)

Population:
It is generally believed that the first living cell came into existence about 3,500 million years ago and the first photosynthetic cells consuming carbon dioxide and evolving oxygen came into existence around 2,800 million years ago. There is ample evidence that the atmosphere during the interval from 3,600 million years ago to 1,900 million years ago was essentially devoid of oxygen. Once oxygen producing photosynthetic cells came into existence and started proliferating, the concentration of oxygen started to increase. It reached to a level of one percent about 600 to 1,000 million years ago and to a level of ten percent about 400 million years ago. [6-8]

Since all of the oxygen came from carbon dioxide as a result of photosynthesis, the concentration of carbon dioxide probably remained unchanged until 1,900 million years ago. Since then the concentration of carbon dioxide should have started to decrease as a result of its conversion into oxygen. It probably continued to decrease until the concentration of oxygen stabilized at about 21% about a few hundred million years ago. The present carbon dioxide concentration is about 0.03%.

Since the population of any species depends upon the availability of food, the population of the Jinns probably trended with the concentration of carbon dioxide in the atmosphere. Since their appearance, their population probably continued to increase until about 1,900 million years ago in a way similar to the way the population of humans is increasing. In fact they must have been the most populous species on the earth around 1,900 million years ago. Since then their population probably started to decrease until the oxygen concentration (and carbon dioxide concentration) leveled off about few hundred million years ago. Since their intellect is only inferior to the humans (see Chapter 5), they must also have been the most dominant species on the earth until the appearance of the humans about one or two million years ago.

Prophet Muhammad[SAW] have stated that every person is accompanied by a bad Jinn (satan) who persuades him to do evil.¹ Since the current population of humans is over six billion, there must be at least six billion bad Jinns in the world. This does not include the good Jinns who also populate the earth. According to the Holy Quran, one good person can handle two bad ones.ᵐ If the level of morality in the world is stable, the ratio of bad to good people should be two. There could be three billion good Jinns in the world. The current Jinn population could be about ten billion.

Summary:
The statements from the Holy Quran and Prophet Muhammad^{SAW} suggest that the Jinns have many of the biological characteristics found in the human being and other animals of cellular origin. They procreate to preserve their species, consume food to maintain their life, and do purposeful work. Since we cannot observe the Jinns and their animals, we cannot tell if they possess highly organized structure. However, the existence of multiple species of their kind, according to the statement of Prophet Muhammad^{SAW}, suggests varying degree of complexity among their kind. They probably appeared soon after the creation of the earth about 4,800 million years ago and were probably the most populace until 1,900 million years ago and most dominant species until the appearance of the humans. Their current population could be about ten billion.

---

¹ Every human being has two houses in his heart. In one house lives an angel and in the other house lives satan (evil Jinn). The angel persuades him to do good deeds and the satan persuades him to do bad deeds. When he is busy remembering God, the satan backs off. When he is not busy in remembrance of God, the satan persuades him to do bad deeds. (quoted from Maarif-ul-Quran and Tafseer-e-Mazhari)⁹

ᵐ For the present God has lightened your (task) for He knows that there is a weak spot in you: but (even so) if there are a hundred of you patient and persevering they will vanquish two hundred and if a thousand they will vanquish two thousand with the leave of God: for God is with those who patiently persevere. (8:66)

Secrets of Angels, Demons, Satan, and Jinns

Chapter 5
The Intellectual Ability of the Jinns

The human being is the most intelligent species we know of. He has the faculties of speaking, hearing, sight, intelligence, and understanding. These characteristics distinguish him from the rest of the animals.[a] The human uniqueness usually centers on the gift of speech: 'our faculty of using signs and symbols to stand for things and then to construct abstract or imaginary worlds beyond the here and now.'[1] It is the most powerful channel of communication in the world of nature. It can carry vastly more information, and at a much higher rate, than any other natural form of communication. Speech enables humans to communicate with their own species and the faculty of reasoning produces experiences. We will now explore the kind of intelligence the Jinns possess.

---

[a] He has created man. He has taught him speech (and intelligence). (55:3-4)

It is He who brought you forth from the wombs of your mothers when you knew nothing; and He gave you hearing (*samaa*) and sight (*absaara*) and intelligence and affection (*afeedatah*) that you may give thanks (to God). (16:78)

It is He who created (*anshaa*) for you (the faculties) of hearing (*samaa*), seeing (*absaara*), feeling, and understanding (*afeedatah*). Little thanks it is you give. (23:78)

It is He who has created you (and made you grow) (*anshaa*), and made (*jaala*) for you the faculties of hearing (*samaa*), seeing (*absaara*), feeling, and understanding (*afeedatah*). Little thanks it is you give. (67:23)

Read (*iqra*)! in the name of Your Lord and Cherisher, who created. Created man out of a (mere) clot of congealed blood. Proclaim! and Your Lord is most bountiful. He who taught (the use of) the Pen - Taught man (*al-insaan*) which he knew not. (96:1-5)

The Power of Communication:

According to Quranic verses, the Jinns, like humans, also seem to possess the power of communication. They communicate with each other and with the human being. They can listen to our conversation and understand it. During the lifetime of Prophet Muhammad[SAW], a group of Jinns passed by him and heard him reading the verses of the Holy Quran. They not only listened to those verses, they also communicated those verses to their people.[b]

As mentioned in Chapter 3, there were Jinns who worked for Prophet Solomon (Sulaiman[AS]). In order to take orders form him, they must have been able to communicate with him. The Holy Quran specifically mentions of a Jinn (*Ifreet*, a powerful Jinn) who conversed with Prophet Solomon (Sulaiman[AS]) in his court.[c]

The statements of Prophet Muhammad[SAW] quoted earlier (References 2-4 of Chapter 4) suggest that the Jinns also conversed with Prophet Muhammad[SAW]. The Jinns can also

---

[b] Behold, We turned towards you a company of Jinns (al-jinn): when they stood in the presence thereof, they said, "Listen in silence!" When the reading was finished, they returned to their people, to warn (them of their sins). They said, "O our people! we have heard a Book revealed after Moses, confirming what came before it: it guides (men) to the Truth and to a Straight path. O our people, hearken to the one who invites (you) to God, and believe in him: He will forgive you your faults, and deliver you from a Penalty Grievous. If any does not hearken to the one who invites (us) to God, he cannot frustrate (God's Plan) on the earth, and no protectors can he have besides God: such men (wander) in manifest error." (46:29-32)

Say: It has been revealed to me that a company (*nafr*) of Jinns (*al-jinn*) listened (to the Quran). They said, "We have really heard a wonderful Recital. It gives guidance to the Right, and we have believed therein: we shall not join (in worship) any (gods) with our Lord. And exalted is the Majesty of our Lord: He has taken neither a wife nor a son. (72:1-3)

[c] Said an *Ifrit* (a large, powerful jinn, reputed to be wicked and crafty), of the Jinns (al-jinn): "I will bring it (the throne of the Queen of Saba) to you before you rise from your council: indeed I have full strength for the purpose, and may be trusted." (27:39)

Secrets of Angels, Demons, Satan, and Jinns

communicate with the human being in general after assuming human form. In the battle of Badr during the time of Prophet Muhammad^{SAW}, Satan (Iblees), a Jinn, assumed the form of Suraaqah ibn Malik, the leader of the tribe of Banu Bakr, and encouraged the Quraish to fight against Muslims.[2,3] The Jinns, specially the evil ones, can also communicate with the humans through thoughts and give them ideas and suggestions.[d]

As mentioned in Chapter 3, the Jinns have strong penetrating power. They can penetrate into the human body through the blood stream. Once in the blood stream they can reach any part of human body and establish communication. The Jinns' understanding of human communication is, however, has some limitations. They could not sense the death of Prophet Solomon (Sulaiman^{AS}) until his body fell down.[e]

The Jinns also have the ability to listen to the communications of the angels.[f]

---

[d] Say: I seek refuge with the Lord and Cherisher of Mankind, the King of Mankind, the God of Mankind from the Whisperer (of evil), who withdraws (after his whisper), (the same) who whispers into the hearts of Mankind - among Jinns and among Men. 114 (1-6)]

Every human being has two houses in his heart. In one house lives an angel and in the other house lives satan (evil Jinn). The angel persuades him to do good deeds and the satan persuades him to do bad deeds. When he is busy remembering God, the satan backs off. When he is not busy in remembrance of God, the satan persuades him to do bad deeds. (quoted from Maarif-ul-Quran and Tafseer-e-Mazhari)[4]

[e] Then We decreed (Solomon's) death, nothing showed them his death except a little worm of the earth, which (slowly) gnawing away at his staff: so when he fell down, the Jinns (al-jinn) saw that if they had known the unseen, they would not have tarried in the humiliating penalty (of their task). (34:14)

[f] And we pried into the secrets of heaven (*as-samaa-a*); but we found it filled with stern guards and flaming fires (*shohoba*). We used, indeed, to sit there in (hidden) stations, to (steal) a hearing; but any who listens now will find a flaming fire (*shihaab*) watching in ambush. And we understand not whether ill is intended to those on the earth, or whether their Lord (really) intends to guide them to right conduct. (72:8-10)

The Jinns' ability to climb up to an altitude of 70 miles also gives them a better view of the events happening on the earth. Their supersonic speed should give them the ability to speedily communicate the events. Prophet Muhammad[SAW] also stated that a normal human being with special skills may also be able to communicate with the Jinns.

Power to Observe:
The Jinns can see us, but we cannot see them.[g] They probably can even see angels. During the battle of Badr, when Satan, a Jinn, saw angels helping the Muslim forces, he ran away.[h]

The interaction between light and molecule is well known. The photosynthesis through which light converts carbon dioxide and water into carbohydrate is the basis of the plant life and therefore all cellular life. A branch of chemistry called photochemistry studies the interaction between molecules and light. Since the Jinns are made from carbon dioxide molecule

---

Some people solicited from Prophet Muhammad[SAW] information about soothsayers (*kahin*). He[SAW] said: They are humbug and nonsense. The companions asked: O Messenger of God! Sometimes they foretell something which comes true. Prophet Muhammad[SAW] explaining this said: That is something true which the Jinn hears by chance from the angels and which he conveys to his colleague, and they mix a hundred falsehoods with it (and tell to the people). (Sahih Bukhari and Sahih Muslim)[5]

Prophet Muhammad[SAW] said: The angels descend into the atmosphere with heavenly orders, talking of something that has been decreed in heaven, and the Satan over-hears this and thereafter communicates it to soothsayers, who add a hundred falsehoods with it themselves (to convey to their clients). (Sahih Bukhari[5])

[g] --- for he (Satan) and his tribe watch you from a position where you cannot see them --- (7:27)

[h] Remember Satan made their (sinful) acts seem alluring to them and said: "No one among men can overcome you this day while I am near to you": but when the two forces came in sight of each other he turned on his heels and said: "Lo! I am clear of you; lo! I see what you see not; lo! I fear God; for God is strict in punishment. (8:48)

and the angels, as will be discussed in Section III, are made from light particles, it is not surprising that the Jinns could hear and see the angels within their sphere of influence (up to an altitude of 60 to 70 miles).

Intelligence:

The Jinns, like humans, also possess intelligence. They use reasoning and observation to draw conclusions. It was only the power of reasoning, though misguided [i], that led Satan, a Jinn, to conclude that he was superior to Adam^{AS}.

According to the verses quoted earlier $^{72(8-10)}$, the Jinns, during the lifetime of Prophet Muhammad^{SAW}, used reasoning to conclude that something important was going on somewhere. They not only investigated the matter, they, after making the correct observation and the conclusion, persuaded their fellow Jinns to accept the new message. $^{46\,(29-32)}$

Satan and evils Jinns use power of persuasion to convince the humans to do bad things. It was Satan's power of persuasion that deceived Adam^{AS} and his wife.[j]

As mentioned earlier, the evil Jinns persuade the humans to do bad things.[4]

Summary:

The Jinns, like humans, have the power of observation and intelligence. They communicate with humans through their thought process and with prophets and people of special skills.

---

[i] (God) said: "What prevented you from bowing down when I commanded you?" He said: "I am better than he (Adam). You did create me from fire, and him from clay." (7:12, also 38:75-76)

[j] Then began Satan to whisper suggestions to them (Adam and his wife), in order to reveal to them their shame that was hidden from them. (Before) he said: "Your Lord only forbade you this tree, lest you should become angels or such beings as live forever." And he swore to them both, that he was their sincere adviser. (7:20-21)

But Satan whispered evil to him (Adam). He said, "O Adam! shall I lead you to the Tree of Eternity and to a kingdom that never decays?" (20:120)

They may also converse directly with the human being after acquiring human form. They can probably see the angels and listen to their conversation.

Chapter 6
The Spiritual Nature of the Jinns

We mentioned in Chapter 1 that the Jinns, like the human being, are conscience being. This makes them a responsible being. In this chapter we will explore their spiritual nature.

Reason for the Creation:
The Holy Quran states that the Jinns, like humans, have been created to serve God.[a]

Free Will:
The Jinns, like humans, have conscience and possess a free will.[b] Humans and the Jinns choose to follow or not to follow their conscience with a free will. Their reward on the Day of Judgment will be based on the choices they made in this life.[c]

Influence on the Human Being:
The Jinns, specially the evil ones, enter human body and run into the blood stream.[5-8] From there they penetrate into all the parts of human body and influence the thought process of the human

---

[a] I have only created Jinns (*al-jinn*) and humans (*al-ins*), that they may serve Me. (51:56)

[b] Amongst us (Jinns) are some that submit their wills (to God), and some that swerve from justice. Now those who submit their wills - they have sought out (the path) of right conduct. (72:14)

[c] And to all are (assigned) degrees according to the deeds which they (have done), and in order that (God) may recompense their deeds and no injustice be done to them. (46:18-19)

If We had so willed, We could certainly have brought every soul its true guidance: But the Word from Me will come true, "I will fill Hell with Jinns (*al-jinnah*) and human being (*al-naas*) all together. (32:13)

being.[d] This topic will be discussed in detail in Chapter 15 (The Power and Influence of Satan).

Who/What Influences the Jinns:
We usually blame Satan for all the evils. But Satan appeared only after the creation of Adam[AS]. We have already made a case that the Jinns were in existence well before the appearance of Satan. A question can be raised that who influences the Jinns to do evil, especially before the appearance of Satan.

Both the humans and the Jinns have self (*nafs*). The self by nature is programmed to preserve its existence in this life. Every living organism does its best to protect itself from dangers, either by fighting the danger or by running away from it. This phenomenon is called 'fight or flight' in biology. In doing so it acts in a selfish manner, which is good to a certain extent. When this nature becomes so dominant that it transgresses all the limits, it becomes evil.[e]

---

[d] Every human being has two houses in his heart. In one house lives an angel and in the other house lives satan (evil Jinn). The angel persuades him to do good deeds and the satan persuades him to do bad deeds. When he is busy remembering God, the satan backs off. When he is not busy in remembrance of God, the satan persuades him to do bad deeds.[9] (Prophet Muhammad[SAW])

[e] That which is on the earth We have made but as a glittering show for the earth, in order that We may test them as to which of them are best in conduct. (18:7)

Know you (all) that the life of this world is but play and amusement, pomp and mutual boasting, and a vying in the multiplication of wealth and children. --- And what is the life of this world, but goods and chattels of deception. (57:20) AYA/MHS

The love of desires, women and sons and hoarded treasures of gold and silver and well-bred horses and cattle and tilth is made to seem fair to men. This is the provision of the life of this world. And God is He with whom is the good goal (of life). (3:14) MHS

The mutual rivalry for piling up (the good things of this world) diverts you (from the more serious things) until you visit the graves. (102:1-2)

Success lies in controlling the self.^f It is the self that drives both the humans and the Jinns to do the evil. In case of humans Satan and the bad Jinns fuel fire to the selfish desire of the self. In case of the Jinns, they only have to fight their selfish desires.

Messengers:
Since the Jinns are required to willingly serve God, they, like the humans, also need guidance.^g The messengers came for both the human being and the Jinns. However, there is a difference of opinion whether the Jinns received messengers of their own kind or the messengers sent to the humans were also messengers to the Jinns. The Holy Quran suggests that Prophet Muhammad^{SAW} was also a prophet to the Jinns.^h In many verses of the Holy Quran the Jinns are addressed directly.^i

---

Whoever desires this world's life and its glitter, We will pay them in full their deeds therein, and they shall not be made to suffer loss in respect of them. They are those for whom there is nothing but fire in the Hereafter, and of no effect are the deeds that they do, and vain is what they do. (11:15-16) AYA/MHS

^f Those who save themselves from the covetousness of their own soul (*nafs*) – they are the ones that achieve prosperity. (59:9, 64:16)

^g "O you assembly of Jinns (*al-jinn*) and men (*al-ins*)! came there not unto you messengers from amongst you, setting forth unto you My signs, and warning you of the meeting of this Day of yours?" They will say: "We bear witness against ourselves." It was the life of this world that deceived them. So against themselves will they bear witness that they reject Faith. (6:130)

^h Say: It has been revealed to me that a company (*nafr*) of Jinns (*al-jinn*) listened (to the Quran). They said, "We have really heard a wonderful Recital! It gives guidance to the Right, and we have believed therein: we shall not join (in worship) any (gods) with our Lord. And exalted is the Majesty of our Lord: He has taken neither a wife nor a son." (72:1-3)

Behold, We turned towards you a company of Jinns (*al-jinn*): when they stood in the presence thereof, they said, "Listen in silence!" When the reading was finished, they returned to their people, to warn (them of

Verse 46(30) also suggests that, like Jews, some of the Jinns in the lifetime of Prophet Muhammad^{SAW}, believed and, therefore, followed the book given to Prophet Moses (Moosa^{AS}). In other words though Prophet Moosa^{AS} was sent to the Children of Israeel, he was also a prophet to the Jinns. By extrapolation we can infer that the messengers sent to a nation of the human being were also prophets to the Jinns living among those nations. The Holy Quran also suggests that only males (*rajl*) came as messengers.[j] This, however, does not rule out Jinn messengers, since the Holy Quran has used the term '*rajl*' for both human and

---

their sins). They said, "O our people! we have heard a Book revealed after Moses, confirming what came before it: it guides (men) to the Truth and to a Straight path. "O our people, hearken to the one who invites (you) to God, and believe in him: He will forgive you your faults, and deliver you from a Penalty Grievous. "If any does not hearken to the one who invites (us) to God, he cannot frustrate (God's Plan) on the earth, and no protectors can he have besides God: such men (wander) in manifest error." (46:29-32)

[i] Say: "If the whole of mankind (*al-ins*) and Jinns (*al-jinn*) were to gather together to produce the like of this Quran they could not produce the like thereof, even if they backed up each other with help and support. (17:88)

Soon shall We settle your affairs O both you worlds (the Jinn and the Human Being). (55:31)

O you assembly of Jinns (*al-jinn*) and men (*al-ins*)! If it be you can pass beyond the zones (*aqtaar*) of the heavens (*as-samaawaat*) and the earth (*al-ardh*), pass you! not without authority (or power) shall you be able to pass. (55:33)

"O you assembly of Jinns (*al-jinn*) and men (*al-ins*)! came there not unto you messengers from amongst you, setting forth unto you My signs, and warning you of the meeting of this Day of yours?" They will say: "We bear witness against ourselves." It was the life of this world that deceived them. So against themselves will they bear witness that they reject Faith. (6:130)

[j] And before you also the apostles We sent were male (*rajl*), to whom We granted inspiration ---- (16:43, 21:7)

Jinn males.[k] As was mentioned in Chapter 4, the Jinns were in existence and were probably the most dominant species before the appearance of humans. It is possible that they could have received Jinn prophet in pre-human era. Since their appearance the humans became the dominant species. It probably became incumbent upon the Jinns to follow the human prophets.

Believers and Unbelievers:
Since the Jinns have free will, it implies that some of them will submit themselves willingly to serve God, while many, using their free will, will follow their own desires.[l] The Jinns informing their people about Prophet Muhammad[SAW] were aware that some will rush to accept the Prophet's invitation and some would not.[m] The Quran also tells us that there are righteous Jinns as well as non-righteous Jinns.[n]

The Quranic verses suggest that some Jinns became Muslim [72(1-2)] and that there were Jewish [46(30)] and *Mushrik* Jinns

---

[k] True, there were persons (*rijal*) among mankind who took shelter with persons (*rijal*) among the Jinns, but they increased them in folly. (72:6)

[l] Amongst us (Jinns) are some that submit their wills (to God), and some that swerve from justice. Now those who submit their wills - they have sought out (the path) of right conduct. (72:14)

[m] "O our people, hearken to the one who invites (you) to God, and believe in him: He will forgive you your faults, and deliver you from a Penalty Grievous. (46:31)

"If any does not hearken to the one who invites (us) to God, he cannot frustrate (God's Plan) on the earth, and no protectors can he have besides God: such men (wander) in manifest error." (46:32)

[n] There are among us (Jinns) some that are righteous, and some the contrary; we follow divergent paths. But we think that we can by no means frustrate God throughout the earth (*al-ardh*) by flight (*harab*). As for us, since we have listened to the guidance, we have accepted it: and any who believes in his Lord has no fear, either of a short (account) or of any injustice. (72:11-13)

72(2). Since some Jinns believed that God could have a wife and son 72(3), there could also be Christian Jinns.

Basic Beliefs of the Believing Jinns:
Since the Jinns are expected to believe in the Holy Quran, the basic belief of the Muslim Jinns should be the same as that of the Muslim human being. The verses cited above suggest that they believe in oneness of God, the prophets and messengers of God, the books of God, and angels. The Holy Quran suggests that they also believe in the Day of Judgment.º

Mischief of the Non-believing Jinns:
The evil Jinns, like the evil humans, are mischievous. The Holy Quran cites some of their mischievous acts:

(a) They obviously follow Satan.

(b) They are the enemy of the Messengers of God.ᵖ One of their strategies in opposing the messengers and the prophets was to put doubts in the minds of people who listened to the message of God.ᑫ

(c) It has already been stated in Chapter 2 that they eavesdrop in the heaven.

º And they (came to) think as you thought, that God would not raise up any one (to Judgment). (72:7)

ᵖ Likewise did We make for every Messenger an enemy - evil ones among humans (*al-ins*) and the Jinns (*al-jinn*), inspiring each other with flowery discourses by way of deception. If your Lord had so planned, they would not have done it: so leave them and their inventions alone. (6:112)

ᑫ Never did We send a messenger or a prophet before you (Muhammad), but, when he did recite the revelation or narrated or spoke, Satan threw (some falsehood) in it. But God abolishes that which Satan throws in. Then God establishes His revelations. And God is All-Knower, All-Wise. (22:52) NQ

(d) It has already been stated in Chapter 5 that they give bad ideas to the humans[114(1-6)].

Post-Death Punishment (Punishment of the Grave):
The Angel of Death visits both the humans and the Jinns. The rebellious ones are joined with the rebellious humans and the Jinns of the past into the Fire where they suffer the punishment of the grave.[r]

Resurrection:
The Jinns, like the human being, are accountable for their deeds.[s] This accountability will take place on the Day of Judgment. They will therefore be resurrected on the Day of Judgment and judged.[t] The non-believing Jinns will be sent to hell.[u]

---

[r] He (Angel of Death) will say: "Enter you in the company of the People who passed away before you - men (al-ins) and jinn (al-jinn) - into the Fire. ---- (7:38)

[s] Soon shall We settle your affairs, O both you worlds (the Jinns and the human being). (55:31)

And to all are (assigned) degrees according to the deeds which they (have done), and in order that (God) may recompense their deeds and no injustice be done to them. (46:19)

[t] One day will He gather them all together, (and say): "O you assembly of Jinns (*al-jinn*)! Much (toll) did you take of men (*al-ins*)." Their friends amongst men will say: "Our Lord! we made profit from each other; but (alas!) we reached our term - which You did appoint for us." He will say: "The Fire be your dwelling therein forever, except as God wills, for your Lord is full of wisdom and knowledge.(6:128)

"O you assembly of Jinns (*al-jinn*) and men (*al-ins*)! came there not unto you messengers from amongst you, setting forth unto you My signs, and warning you of the meeting of this Day of yours?" They will say: "We bear witness against ourselves." It was the life of this world that deceived them. So against themselves will they bear witness that they reject Faith. (6:130)

On that Day No question will be asked of man (*ins*) or Jinn (*jaann*). (55:39)

Although the Holy Quran does not categorically state that the believing Jinns will go to paradise, it does mention that those who believe and do good deeds would have a reward that will never fail.[v] The Holy Quran states that the reward for good

---

(For) the sinners will be known by their Marks: and they will be seized by their forelocks and their feet. (55:41)

[u] If We had so willed, We could certainly have brought every soul its true guidance: But the Word from Me will come true, "I will fill Hell with Jinns (*al-jinnah*) and men (*al-naas*) all together. (32:13)

And We have destined for them intimate companions (of like nature), who made alluring to them what was before them and behind them; and the sentences among the previous generations of Jinns (*al-jinn*) and men (*al-ins*), who have passed away, is proved against them; for they are utterly lost. (41:25)

And the Unbelievers will say: "Our Lord! Show us those among Jinns (*al-jinn*) and men (*al-ins*), who misled us: we shall crush them beneath our feet, so that they become the vilest (before all). (41:29)

Many are the Jinns (*al-jinn*) and men (*al-ins*) We have made for Hell: They have hearts wherewith they understand not, eyes wherewith they see not, and ears wherewith they hear not. They are like cattle - no more misguided: for they are heedless (of warning). (7:179)

Except those on whom your Lord has bestowed His Mercy: and for this did He create them: and the Word of your Lord will be fulfilled: "I will fill Hell with jinns (*al-jinnah*) and men (*an-naas*) all together." (11:119)

[v] For those who believe and work deeds of righteousness is a reward that will never fail. (41:8), 84:25)

And to all are (assigned) degrees according to the deeds which they (have done), and in order that (God) may recompense their deeds, and no injustice be done on them. (48:19)

God has promised those among them who believe and do righteous deeds Forgiveness and a great reward. (48:29)

is good.[w] Reward and punishment are intertwined in the court of God. Where there is punishment for bad deeds, there is reward for good deeds. For example, the wives of Prophet Muhammad[SAW] were told in the Holy Quran[x] that their punishment will double for lewdness and their reward will also double for being submissive to God and Prophet Muhammad[SAW]. Hence God will reward the Jinns who believe and do good deeds. It is contrary to Wisdom and Justice of God[y] that whereas the unbelieving Jinns will go to hell, the believing Jinns will not go to paradise. Whereas hell is made for punishment, paradise is made for reward. The only way to reward the Jinns will be a place in paradise.[z]

Summary:
The spiritual nature of the Jinns is very similar to the humans. They are created to worship God. They have been given free will to choose between their conscience and selfish desired. Whereas

---

[w] Is there any Reward for Good -- other than Good? (55:60)

[x] O Consorts of the Prophet! if any of you were guilty of evident unseemly conduct, the punishment would be doubled to her, and that is easy for God.

But any of you that is devout in the service of God and His Messenger, and works righteousness - to her shall We grant her reward twice and We have prepared for her a generous Sustenance. (33:30-31)

[y] For those who reject God, is a terrible Penalty. But for those who believe and work righteous deeds, is Forgiveness, and a magnificent Reward. (35:7)

[z] Soon shall We settle your affairs, O both you worlds (the Jinns and the human being). (55:31)

In them (the two Gardens) will be (Maiden), chaste, restraining their glances, whom no human (*ins*) or Jinn (*Jaann*) has touched. (55:56)

In them will be fair (Companions), good, beautiful. --- Companions restrained (as to their glances), in goodly pavilions. --- Whom no human (*ins*) or Jinn (*Jaann*) before them has touched. (55:70-74)

both their selfish desires and Satan influence humans, the Jinns are only influenced by their selfish desires to do evil. Like humans, they also receive guidance. The prophets who came to humans were also prophet for the Jinns. They are expected to believe in the same things the humans are expected to believe in. All kinds of religion that exist among the human being also exist among the Jinns. They will suffer post-death punishment, will be resurrected, will be accountable for their deeds, and will be rewarded accordingly on the Day of Judgment.

Chapter 7
The Jinns and the Humans

It was stated in the previous chapter that the spiritual nature of the Jinns and the human being are almost the same. Both of them are created to worship God, have been given free will and conscience, received guidance, will be accountable for their deeds, and will be rewarded accordingly on the Day of Judgment. In this chapter we will discuss the difference between the two, some of which have already been highlighted in previous chapters.

Different Origin and State:
It has already been stated that the Jinns and the human being are of different origin. The Jinns are of gaseous origin and the human being is of cellular origin. Due to the difference in origin, the Jinns exhibit the characteristics of gas and the human exhibit the characteristics of solid. The Jinns are therefore invisible, imperceptible, highly penetrable, and flexible in size and shape. The human being does not possess these characteristics.

Both Inhabit the Planet Earth:
Although the Jinns and the humans exist in two different states, both inhabit the planet earth.[a]

Created before the Human Being:
The Holy Quran states that the Jinn race was created before the human being.[b]

---

[a] But we (the Jinns) think that we can by no means frustrate God throughout the earth nor can we frustrate Him by flight. (72:12)

[b] And the Jinn race (*Al-Jaann*), We had created before, from the fire of a scorching wind. (15:27)

A statement of Prophet Muhammad[SAW] also suggests that the Jinns were created before the human being.[1] Based on the evidence[2-4], we stated in Chapter 4 that the Jinns were probably created soon after the creation of the earth about 4,800 million years ago. Humans came into existence within the last two million years.

Inferior to the Human Being:
The human being is the vicegerent of God on this earth.[c] They are the best of the creatures.[d] All the things in the heaven and the earth are subjected to them.[e] It is the superiority of the human being over the Jinns that was unacceptable to Satan, one of the Jinns.[f] As mentioned in Chapter 4, the Jinns were probably the most dominant species on the earth before the appearance of the humans. Satan refused to accept this demotion and rebelled (See Section III).

Power of Communication:
It has already been stated in Chapter 5 that the Jinns communicate among themselves. They also have the ability to see and listen to the human and the angels (within 70 miles of altitude). They can also communicate with them through thought

---

[c] Behold, Your Lord said to the angels: "I will create a vicegerent on the earth." (2:30)

[d] We have indeed created human being in the best of moulds. (95:4)

And (He) has given you shape, and made your shapes beautiful – (40:64), 64:3)

[e] Do you not see that God has subjected to your (use) all the things in the heavens and on the earth, and has made his bounties flow to you in exceeding measure, (both) seen and unseen. (31:20)

[f] Behold We said to the angels: "Bow down unto Adam." They bowed down except Iblees. He said: "Shall I bow to one whom You have created from clay. He said: "Tell me, is this the one who You have honored above me. If You will give me respite until the Day of Judgment, I will surely bring his descendent under my sway, all but few." (17:61-62)

Secrets of Angels, Demons, Satan, and Jinns

process or by acquiring human form. Humans cannot see or listen to the angels or the Jinns. It was also stated that only prophets and the human being with special skills can communicate with the Jinns.[10]

Speed:

Compared to the Jinns, whose average speed is about 850 miles per hour, the average speed of the human being is only 3-5 miles per hour. However, by utilizing the knowledge given by God, the human being has developed modes of transportation (Table 1) which has increased their speed. By training horses, they increased their speed to 40 miles per hour.[11] By inventing train and automobiles their speed increased to 250 miles per hour.[12,13] By inventing jet plane their speed reached 530 miles per hour.[14] By developing supersonic jets their speed approached 1,500 to 2,000 miles per hour.[14,15] Finally by mastering the rocket technology, they can travel at a speed of 25,000 miles per hour.[16,17] This has given them a big edge over the Jinns. It was a human being who, by the knowledge given by God, was able to bring the throne of the Queen of Saba in the court of Prophet Solomon (Sulaiman[AS]) in the blink of an eye.[g] Assuming that the blink of an eye takes less than a second, this translates into a speed of more than 3,000 miles per second which is about one-sixtieth of the speed of light (186,000 miles per second).[18]

Space Adventure:

According to the Holy Quran, space travel by the Jinns and the human being is possible if they have authority (*sultaan*).[h]

---

[g] Said one who had knowledge of the Book: "I will bring it to you within the twinkling of an eye!" Then when (Solomon) saw it placed firmly before him, he said: "This is by the grace of my Lord! - to test me whether I am grateful or ungrateful! and if any is grateful, truly his gratitude is (a gain) for his own soul; but if any is ungrateful, truly my Lord is Free of All Needs, Supreme in Honor! (27:40)

[h] O you assembly of Jinns (*al-jinn*) and men (*al-ins*)! If it be you can pass beyond the zones (*aqtaar*) of the heavens (*as-samaawaat*) and the earth (*al-ardh*), pass you! not without authority shall you be able to pass. (55:33)

51

The verses suggest that space adventurer will encounter shooting stars (*shwaaz*) and suffocation *(Noohaas)*. Although we do not know if suffocation is an issue for the Jinns, but we do know from the Quranic verses that they encounter shooting stars, which limits their access to the space up to an altitude of 60 to 70 miles.

The case of space adventure for the human being has taken a new meaning. Although they themselves cannot fly, but by mastering the rocket technology, they have been able to free themselves from the earth's gravity. Since air is in scarcity at higher altitude, suffocation was an issue for them. However, by mastering chemistry and handling of compressed gases, they have been able to overcome this hurdle too.

The term '*noohaas*' has also been translated as molten brass or copper.[19] The Quranic statement would then imply that if the humans adventure in the space, they will encounter a temperature where copper will be in molten form. The space shuttle and rockets experience a temperature of about 2,700 degrees Fahrenheit when escaping or entering the earth's atmosphere due to friction of the air.[20] This temperature is above the melting temperature of copper (2,000 degrees Fahrenheit),[21] but below the melting temperature of Iron (2,800 degrees Fahrenheit).[21] By mastering the metallurgy, the humans have developed materials that can protect them and their vehicle from such intense heat and has enabled them to travel to moon. The Jinns on the other hand are still limited to the zone of meteoritic activity (an altitude of 60 to 70 miles).

Intelligence Gathering:
The Jinns' ability to travel at about 850 miles per hour up to an altitude of 70 miles gave them an advantage in gathering and communicating information over the humans in pre-space age. The humans, by mastering rocket and satellite technology, have surpassed the Jinns in speed as well as in their ability to climb higher altitude. They can transmit and receive information at the speed of light, which is much faster than the speed of the Jinns.

On you will be sent (O you evil ones twain!) a flame of fire (to burn) (*showaaz*) and a smoke (to choke) (*noohaas*): no defense will you have. (55:35)

The weather satellites orbit the earth every twelve hours at an altitude of 18,200 miles and communicate weather conditions of the globe. The communication satellites orbit the earth every twenty four hours at an altitude of 22,300 miles and transmit TV and telephone signals to different parts of the world.[22] The Jinns, however, have the ability to listen to the communications of the angels, which the humans cannot do.

Power:
As mentioned in Chapter 3, the Jinns consume food to provide themselves energy. Being of gaseous nature, the Jinns could use this energy do purposeful work. The humans, by mastering the combustion technology, have been able to generate more power than the Jinns. They have developed turbines, internal combustion engine, jet engine, and rocket engines. They have been able to produce electricity and operate machinery, automobiles, trains, aircraft, and rockets.[23] They have mastered the travel in land and air at supersonic speed. They have also overcome the gravitational pull of the earth and have traveled in the space, far beyond the capability of the Jinns.

Transformation:
As mentioned in the previous chapters, the Jinns have the ability to acquire human or other animal form. The humans do not have such capability due to their state.

Mass:
Compared to the size of a cell, which ranges between 10 to 100 microns[24], the size of the carbon dioxide molecule is about 0.002 microns.[25] One micron is one millionth of a meter. The size of the basic building block of molecular life form could therefore be about 5,000 to 50,000 times smaller than the basic building block of cellular life form. The weight of an average human adult is in the range of about 70 to 90 kilograms (150 to 200 pounds) and has more than 100 trillion cells.[26] We do not know the mass of the Jinns or how many carbon dioxide molecules are there in his body, but comparing the mass of the cell with carbon dioxide molecule suggests that the mass of human being will be

10 to 10,000 trillion times more than the Jinns. The comparison is shown in Table 2.

Summary:

The Jinns are invisible, imperceptible, highly penetrable, and flexible in size and shape. The human being does not possess these characteristics. This is due to the difference in the origin of the two. The Jinns, though created before the human being, are inferior to the humans. The humans have overcome the advantage the Jinns had in power, speed, and space travel through technological development. The Jinns can see and listen to the communications of the human being and the angels. The bad Jinns can even influence the humans through their thought process. In general the human being cannot see or listen to the conversation of the Jinns or the angels. Prophets and the human being with special skills can communicate with the Jinns. The Jinns have the ability to transform into human and other animals. Humans do not have such ability.

TABLE 1

Speeds of Modes of Transportation

The Human Being	3-5 miles per hour
Race Horse[11]	40 miles per hour
Fastest Train[12]	186 miles per hour
Race Cars[13]	250 miles per hour
Jet Airliners[14]	530 miles per hour
Concord Jet[15]	1,550 miles per hour
Combat Aircraft[14]	2,000 miles per hour
Space Shuttle[16]	17,500 miles per hour
Rocket[17]	25,000 miles per hour
Light[18]	670 million miles per hour
Sound[27]	761 miles per hour

Table 2

A Comparison of the Jinns with the Human Being

	Human Being	The Jinns
State	Solid	Gas
Shape	Fixed	Flexible
Size	Fixed	Flexible
Basic Building Block	Cell	Molecule
Size of the Basic Building Block	10 – 100 microns	0.002 microns
Mass of the Basic Building Block	6×10^{-7} to 6×10^{-10} gm	7×10^{-23} gm
Ratio of the Basic Building Block Volume	5,000 – 50,000	1
Ratio of Basic Building Block Mass	10 trillion to 10,000 trillion	1

Chapter 8
Deriving Benefits from the Jinns

We mentioned in Chapter 7 that human being is the vicegerent of God on the earth. It is because of this status that everything in the universe has been subjugated to him.[a] It is because of this authority that humans have been able to derive benefits form other creations of God. Deriving benefit, however, requires mastery. Unless we tame or domesticate the animals, we cannot use them for our benefit. Even space technology, as mentioned in the previous chapter, required mastery of many other technologies. The verse implies that humans can even derive benefits from the Jinns. Based on the nature of the Jinns described in the previous chapters, we will now discuss some of the benefits that can be derived from the Jinns.

Intelligence Gathering:
Since the Jinns are invisible and imperceptible, they could help gather intelligence. Their sonic speed and ability to climb higher altitude could be an asset for this purpose. They can be sent to strategic locations and sites to listen, observe, and communicate, without spending millions on spy satellites and drones.

Weather Forecasting:
The Jinns with their speed and ability to climb higher altitude may be able to provide weather report, without spending millions on weather satellites.

Investigation of Crime:
The invisibility and imperceptibility of the Jinns may also help investigate crimes. Many times it is hard to locate the evidence to prove the case against criminals. They may be able to help the investigators fetch this information.

---

[a] Do you not see that God has subjected to your (use) all the things in the heavens and on the earth, and has made his bounties flow to you in exceeding measure, (both) seen and unseen. (31:20)

Transportation and Delivery:
Their speed and access to a higher altitude gives them the ability to transport objects to distant places in short time.

Diagnosis in Health Care:
The Jinns, being of gaseous nature, are highly penetrable. They may be able to penetrate the human body and investigate the ailment. They can be used in place of X-ray, MRI and other diagnostic tools. The author has heard of one case history where the Jinns assisted in the diagnosis of a disease.

Cancer Treatment:
The penetrability of the Jinns may also help in diagnosis and treatment of cancer. They may be able to penetrate inside the human body and locate the cancerous cell. They may also be able to destroy those particular cells.

Diagnosis in Manufacturing Industry:
In manufacturing industry, many times entry into equipment is required to diagnose the cause of malfunction. For example plugging and misplacement of trays in distillation towers, equipment breakdown, and etc. The Jinns may be able to creep into the equipment and may be able to diagnose the problem.

Summary:
The gaseous nature of the Jinns may allow humans to benefit from them in intelligence gathering, weather forecasting, crime investigation, transportation and delivery of objects, diagnosis in health care and manufacturing industry, and cancer treatment.

Only by understanding their nature and establishing communication with them, humans would be able to derive benefits from them. It is the understanding of the author that it is possible to establish communication with them, but like anything else, it requires certain technique and expertise. By establishing research institutions where people who possess expertise of communicating with the Jinns develop the techniques to derive benefits from them. Unfortunately technology is a double-edged sword. It can be used to benefit humankind or to harm them. Nuclear technology has been used both to generate power as well as to annihilate humans in mass number. The author has heard stories where people who had control over the Jinns used them for stealing and other unethical activities. Safeguards must be in place before developing this technology.

Chapter 9
Myths about the Jinns

There are many myths about the Jinns. In view of the new understanding about the Jinns, the author is addressing some of these myths in this chapter.

Haunted Houses:
Sometimes when a house remains unoccupied for an extended period of time, it becomes haunted. It has been said that it is occupied by the Jinns. There have been cases where a new human occupant experiences weird things when he moves into such a house[1]. Imagine yourself sitting in your living room and the pots and pans start flying all around you. Naturally you will try to duck. Or imagine yourself sitting on a sofa, and the sofa starts to lift up in air. Some people tough it out and some end up vacating the house. In some cases, the situation was resolved by experts who could communicate with the Jinns. In such cases the human and the Jinn residents agreed to share the house. A portion of the house was left vacant for the Jinns.

It is understandable that, like the human being, the Jinns also have families and need some privacy. Being made of gas, they also need some space. It is very much possible that when a house remains vacant for an extended period, the Jinns take occupation of that house. Since the Jinns are invisible, a new human occupant may not notice their presence and moves in. This will infringe upon the privacy of the Jinn occupant. Considering themselves a rightful owner of the house, they will do anything to evict the new human occupant.

Dirty Tricks:
Just like the human being, the Jinns also have children and like our kids, some of them may also be naughty. Imagine you living in a house, where the Jinns are giving you company. Let us say they are living in your attic. Once in a while their kid may wander into your kitchen and start playing with your pots and

pans. They may start using those pots and pans as ball or frisbee. I will not blame you if you get scared. But it is only a game for them. Or you may hear some noise in your attic. Their children may be playing. So as long as they do not bother you, there is no need for you to bother them.

Some times naughty Jinns may pull naughty tricks, for example[1]:

> The light switch automatically turning on and off;
> Knock on the door, without anybody being present;
> Things missing;
> Shower of stones;
> Automatic opening and closing of doors;
> People walking in the attic;
> Sound of music;
> Flying of pots, pans, crockery, and utensils;
> Furniture rising up in the air;
> Shower of human bones;
> Scattering of human feces

Knowing that the Jinns are invisible, but have the power to move objects, it is understandable that they can pull these tricks. Although they are not supposed to bother human being, but just like human being, there are bad Jinns who may violate this rule and bother us. Sometimes they do these things when, as mentioned above, their privacy has been violated.

Jinns have no shadow:
It has been said that even when the Jinns acquire human or animal form, they do not have shadow. There may be some truth to this myth. Being made of gases, they are not as dense as the humans, who are made from solid substances. When light ray falls on a solid surface, it is blocked by the solid body, casting a shadow behind it. Although we do not understand the full nature of the transformation of the Jinns into a human or animal body, let us assume that they give us an outer appearance of a body, but the body like a balloon is full of gases. In such case the shadow will be very faint. Since we are used to seeing a shadow

of solid body, the shadow of balloon type object will give the appearance of no shadow.

Tens of Feet Long Arm:
There have been reports that the Jinns, who live among humans in human form, do things, which is contrary to human experience. The author has heard many stories in which students attending seminary observed one of the students, lying in bed, extended his hand tens of feet to turn off the light switch. As explained earlier, being made of gases, the Jinns have lot of flexibility in size and shape. It is possible that, though their outer appearance was that of a human being, their body is full of gas like a balloon. In balloons the air can be pushed around to give the balloon different shape. This will allow them to extend their arm tens of feet without much of an effort. In the situation described above, probably they forgot that they are posing as human being, and resorted to their natural instinct.

They Walk or Float:
Assuming that in human form, they give the appearance of a human being, but in reality their body, like a balloon, is filled with gases. If this is the case, then they will be very light, and like a balloon, they will in reality be floating, not walking.

Being Possessed:
There are stories about people being possessed by the Jinns. According to the Holy Quran a touch by Satan can cause mental ailment, as it will happen to people who devour usury.[a] The activity of brain is very complex psychological phenomenon and requires a delicate electrical and chemical balance. We know that a sudden financial or emotional disaster or shock sometimes causes humans to suffer heart attack or cause them to go crazy. People who are familiar with the Holy Quran know that

---

[a] Those who devour usury will not stand except as stands one whom Satan by his touch has driven to madness. This is because they say: "Trade is like usury." (2:275)

emotional and financial loses are test of God.[b] So they remain cool in case they suffer any calamity. People, who give up the remembrance of God, become materialistic and are mentally (psychologically) unprepared to handle calamities.[c]

Being made from gases, the Jinns have very high penetrative power and could be able to penetrate the brain. Those who give up the remembrance of God, lose His protection. The evil Jinns may then be able to disturb electrical and chemical balance in the brain, which could give the appearance of being possessed.

Why Do We not Encounter the Jinns Now?
The author has heard many stories from the past where people encountered the Jinns. But such stories or events are rare now. Obviously, with scientific development the superstitious beliefs have almost disappeared. But there could be another reason. As mentioned under the section of the Haunted Houses, the Jinns

---

[b] O You who believe! Seek help with patient Perseverance and Prayer, for God is with those who patiently persevere. -----. Be sure We shall test you with something of fear and hunger, some loss in goods or lives or fruits (of your toil). Give glad tidings to those who patiently persevere - who say, when afflicted with calamity: "To God we belong, and to Him is our return." They are those on whom (descends) blessings from their Lord, and Mercy, and they are the ones who receive guidance. (2:153, 155-157)

[c] Man does not weary of asking for good (things), but if ill touches him, he gives up all hope (and) is lost in despair. (41:49)

If We give man a taste of mercy from Ourselves, and then withdraw it form him, behold! He is in despair and (falls into) blasphemy. But if We give him a taste of (Our) favors after adversity has touched him, he is sure to say, "All evil has departed from me." Behold! He falls into exultation and pride. Not so do those who show patience and constancy, and work righteousness. (11:9-11)

When trouble touches a man, he cries unto Us (in all postures) – lying down, on his side, or sitting, or standing. But when We have solved his trouble, he passes on his way as if he had never cried to Us for a trouble that touched him! (10:11)

prefer uninhabited and dark places. In the pre-electricity era, although people lived in big houses and castles, they used only a small section of the house. Even there they used portable candles for lighting. The rest of the house used to remain dark and uninhabited, which is very inviting for the Jinns. With the development of electricity and increase in population, most of the area in a house is lighted and occupied. The increase in human population, increased lighted area, and cutting down of forests may be causing housing shortage for the Jinns.

Chapter 10
Genie in the Bottle – An Analysis

One of the tales of the famous "Tales of a Thousand and One Nights" titled "The Story of the Fisherman and the Genie" talks about an encounter between a fisherman and a Jinn. In view of our scientific understanding about the Jinns, we will analyze this story and determine how close the creator of the story came to the real nature of the Jinns.

The gist of the story[1] is that when an aged fisherman cast his net, after three unsuccessful and devastating attempts, he netted an empty vessel of yellow copper. When he opened the vessel, a very thick smoke came out and formed a huge mist. 'The smoke ascended to the clouds, and, extending itself along the sea and upon the shore, formed a great mist.'[1] When all the smoke came out, it collected together and formed a giant body, almost twice as high as the tallest human the fisherman had ever seen. It was a genie, whom, according to the story, Prophet Solomon (Sulaiman[AS]) had imprisoned in the vessel. Since it was a bad genie, he started giving the fisherman hard time. So the fisherman tricked the genie in going back to the vessel. The genie's body dissolved, changed itself into smoke, and reentered the vessel. The fisherman then capped the vessel and threw it in the ocean.

The story suggests that the Jinn in the gaseous form was compressed into the vessel. When the fisherman opened the vessel, the Jinn decompressed itself out of the vessel. He then transformed himself into a human body. Later the process took place in reverse. The Jinn transformed back into the gaseous form and compressed itself into the vessel. Excluding the reference to smoke from the story, it is amazing how close the creator of the story came to the real nature of the Jinns. He or she understood that the Jinns exist in gaseous state, which is remarkable, considering how old the story is.

Chapter 11
Summary

The life form we are familiar with is of cellular origin. This includes animals, plants, fungi, protista, and monera. The cell is their basic building block, which contains about 70 to 80 percent water and 20 to 30 percent solid substances such as organic compounds and minerals. The human being is the most complex and most intelligent being of this life form. The Holy Quran informs us about the existence of another class of intelligent being called the Jinns who are made from fire.

    An analysis of fire, how it is created, what comes out of it, and the Quranic description of the creation of the Jinns, suggests that the Jinns are made from gases that are produced from the fire. These gases consist of carbon dioxide and water vapor. The Jinns are probably made from carbon dioxide gases. Based on the gaseous origin of the Jinns, many of his physical characteristics are predicted which matches with the Quranic description. His biological characteristics, intellectual ability, and the spiritual nature are also discussed.

    Whereas the human being is of cellular origin made from solid organic substances and water, the Jinns are of molecular origin made from gases. In fact the statements of Prophet Muhammad^{SAW} suggest that there could be a host of living organisms of molecular gaseous origin. Just as the human being is the most complex and most intelligent being of cellular life form, the Jinns are probably the most complex and most intelligent being of molecular gaseous life form. Both, the human being, from among the cellular beings, and the Jinns, from among the gaseous beings, are given free will and are made responsible for their actions.

    The gaseous nature of the Jinns makes them invisible, imperceptible, and penetrative. It gives them great power and flexibility in size and shape. They can travel at an average speed of about 850 miles per hour, and can fathom space up to an altitude of about 60 to 70 miles. The human being, by technological development, has overcome the advantage the Jinns had in power, speed, and space travel. Probably the Jinns have the ability to inhale and exhale solid, liquid, and gas. This with their flexibility in size and shape will allow them to acquire human and other animal forms. This will also allow them to rise up in the sky by inhaling air.

The statements from the Holy Quran and Prophet Muhammad^{SAW} suggest that the Jinns have many of the same biological characteristics possessed by the cellular beings (human being and animals). They procreate, consume food, and do purposeful work. They were probably created soon after the creation of the earth about 4,800 million years ago. They were probably the most dominant species on the earth until the appearance of the humans. The Jinns, like humans, have also been given the power of observation, intelligence, free will, conscience, and guidance. They are also created to worship God and are expected to believe in the same things the human being is expected to believe in. They will suffer post-death punishment, will be resurrected, will be accountable for their deeds, and will be rewarded accordingly on the Day of Judgment. Probably all kinds of religions that exist among the human being also exist among the Jinns. Though they were created before the human being, they are inferior to him.

Although the Jinns and the human being inhabit the same planet, the two live in two different worlds. Whereas the world of the human being is of solid state, the world of the Jinns is of gaseous state. Being made from colorless gas, the human being cannot see them, but they can see the human being. By the same token, they can listen to human conversation, but the human being cannot listen to their conversation. The interaction between the Jinns and the humans is very limited. They, specially the bad ones, can put ideas and suggestions in human thoughts. They can also converse with the human being after acquiring human form. Only prophets and the human being with special skills can converse with the Jinns. They can probably also see the angels and listen to their conversation.

Considering the gaseous nature of the Jinns, we may be able to benefit from them in intelligence gathering, weather forecasting, crime investigation, transportation and delivery of objects, diagnosis in health care and manufacturing industry, and cancer treatment. It will, however, require, establishing communication with them. There are people who possess this expertise.

There are many myths about the Jinns. Most of these myths can be explained in terms of their characteristics. The analysis of one of the famous stories from "Tales of a Thousand and One Nights" titled "The Story of the Fisherman and the Genie" suggests that the creator of the story understood the true nature of the Jinns.

SECTION II

SATAN

Chapter 12
Who is Satan?

The name Satan is a term of Islamic-Judeo-Christian origin and stands for the Devil. In Islamic-Judeo-Christian tradition Satan is a being who is the instigator of all evil acts. The Arabic equivalent of Satan is *Shaytan*. In the Holy Quran the term '*shaytan*' has been used both, with and without a definite article: *shaytan* and *al-shaytan (*pronounced as *ash-shaytan)*. The term '*shaytan*' or '*al-shayateen*' (the plural of *al-shaytan)* usually stands for being or beings exhibiting evil characteristic.[a] However, the term *al-shaytan* is used for a particular being who refused to bow to Adam[AS], when he was ordered to do so by God.[b] The proper name of that particular being was Iblees. The

---

[a] We have guarded them (heaven) from every evil (*shaytan*) spirit accursed. (15:17)

We have indeed decked the lower heaven with beauty (in) the stars – and for guard against all obstinate rebellious spirit (*shaytan*). (37:6-7)

And yet among men there are such as dispute about God, without knowledge, and follow every evil (*shaytan*) one obstinate in rebellion. (22:3)

They followed what the evil ones (*al-shayateen*) gave out (falsely). (2:102)

Likewise did We make for every messenger an enemy – evil ones (*al-shayateen*) among men and Jinns ---- (6:112)

[b] Then We bade the angels bow down to Adam and they bowed down; not so Iblis. (2:34, 7:11, 15:30-31, 17:61, 18:50, 20:116, 38:73-74)

He was one of the Jinns, and he broke the command of his Lord. (18:50)

He refused to be of those who bow down. He was haughty and became

literal meaning of Iblees is the one who is disappointed. He is given the title of Satan for his evil characteristics. The focus of this section is Iblees, Satan (*al-shaytan*).

The first time we are introduced to Satan in the Holy Quran is when he refused to bow to Adam^{AS}.$^{(2:34)}$ The Holy Quran does not give any past history of Satan, except that he was one of the Jinns, who were created before the human being.^{c} The fact that Satan was one of the Jinns is further confirmed by Iblees himself. He claimed his superiority over Adam^{AS} because he was made from fire and Adam^{AS} was made from clay.^{d} According to the Holy Quran, it is the Jinns who are made from fire.^{e} We can therefore state with certainty that Satan was one of the Jinns, a class of beings made from fire that were in existence before the creation of Adam^{AS}.

---

one of those who reject Faith. (2:34, 7:11, 15:30-31, 17:61, 20:116, 38:73-74)

^{c} Behold! We said to the angels, " Bow down to Adam." They bowed, except Iblees. He was one of the Jinns and he broke the command of his Lord --- (18:50)

And the Jinn race, We had created before, form the fire of a scorching wind. (15:27)

^{d} --- You created me from fire, and him (Adam) from clay. (7:12, 38:76)

^{e} And He created Jinns from fire free of smoke. (55:15)

Chapter 13
Satan and the Jinns

We made a case in the previous chapter that Satan is one of the Jinns. He will, therefore possess the same characteristics as the rest of the Jinns. He should also be a gaseous being. He is probably made from carbon dioxide gas. His physical, biological, and intellectual ability should be the same as that of the Jinns. These characteristics have been discussed in detail in the previous section. However, being Satan, he also possesses some special characteristics. In the next few chapters we will discuss specific characteristics of Satan.

Satan's Headquarter:
Satan being of physical origin must occupy some space. So where is his physical residence? As mentioned earlier, both, the human being and the Jinns, have been challenged in the Holy Quran to dare cross the limits of the earth's atmosphere. It would imply that Satan, one of the Jinns, must be located somewhere on the planet earth. The Holy Quran also quotes a statement by the Jinns that they could not frustrate God throughout the earth, again implying that they are the inhabitants of the earth.[a] As mentioned earlier, both, the human being and the Jinns, are called '*thaqalan*,' which means the beings who gravitate towards the earth.

According to Prophet Muhammad[SAW], the headquarter of Satan is upon the ocean.[b] Since humans mostly live on land, the

---

[a] But we think that we can by no means frustrate God throughout the earth, nor can we frustrate him by flight. (72:12)

[b] The throne of Iblis is upon the ocean and he sends detachments (to different parts) in order to put people to trial and the most important figure in his eyes is one who is most notorious in sowing the seed of dissension. (Muslim: 6754)

Iblis places his throne upon water. He then sends detachments (for

Jinns cannot count on having much privacy on land. Ocean covers about 70 percent of the earth's surface and is mostly uninhabited by humans. It is, therefore, one area where the Jinns can count on having some privacy. Satan, who has taken upon himself to misguide all the humans all the time, must need a location from where he could operate undisturbed and unhindered. Ocean should, therefore, be the most suitable location for his headquarter.

Since the circumference of the earth is about 24,000 miles, it will take a Jinn about twenty eight hours at a speed of 850 miles per hour to make a return trip from the farthest point on the earth to Satan's headquarter. Satan does not need to run a Monte Carlo simulation to determine an optimum location for his headquarter. Since most of the human population is concentrated in Asian continent (mostly in China and Indian subcontinent), his headquarter should be located near India and China. Considering that most of the turmoil is happening in the Middle East, it is a safe bet to suggest that his headquarter is currently located in the Arabian Sea in the Indian Ocean. This will gives him close access to Indian subcontinent, China, and the Middle East. His agents are busy traveling back and forth from his headquarter to all the locations in the world to spread mischief.

Death:

In the previous section we suggested that the Jinns, like the humans, must also suffer death. Most of the Jinns, like the human being, probably have a limited life span. Satan is, however, an exception. He will also die, but not until the end of the world. God has specially granted him a long life span. When he disobeyed God's order to bow to Adam[AS], he challenged God

---

creating dissension). The nearer to him in rank are those who are most notorious in creating dissension. One of them comes and says: I did so and so. And he says: You have done nothing. Then one amongst them comes and says: I did not spare so and so until I sowed the seed of discord between a husband and wife. The Satan goes near him and says: You have done well. He then embraces him. (Muslim: 6755)

that His newly created species (the human being) is unworthy of the status granted to him.[c]

He wanted to have the opportunity to misguide them and prove his point. For this reason he wanted to live until the end of the world.[d] God granted him his wish.[e] Since Satan was present at the time of creation of Adam[AS], his age should at least be the age of the humanity. He could be two million years old.

---

[c] He (Satan) said: "See You? This is the one whom You have honored above me! If You will but respite me to the Day of Judgement, I will surely bring his descendants under my sway – all but a few." (17:62)

[d] He said: "Give me respite till the day they are raised up." (God) said: "Be you amongst those who have respite." (7:14-15)

[e] (God) said: "Be you amongst those who have respite." (7:15)

Chapter 14
The Psychological Nature of Satan

In this chapter we will explore Satan's psychological nature.

Reason for Satan's Creation:
Accountability is an essential feature of human life. In one form or another, we are all conscience of the consequences of our actions. Most of our behavior and relationship is driven by this awareness. Only God is unafraid of the consequences of His actions.[a] Even the rulers, autocratic or democratic, gauge the effect of their decisions on their constituency and make necessary changes to appease them. The CEOs of company watch the stock prices and take necessary actions to make the shareholders happy. Ultimately we will all have to account for our actions on the Day of Judgement. Many of us, however, get carried away in the materialistic life and ignore this reality. The purpose of creating Satan was to distinguish those who believe in the Hereafter (concept of accountability) from those who ignore or reject this reality.[b] Lifestyle of those who remain conscious of this reality is much different from those who reject this reality.

Satan has a Free Will:
Like any other Jinn or human being, Satan has conscience and possesses a free will.[c] Humans and the Jinns choose to follow or not to follow their conscience with a free will. Their reward on

---

[a] And for Him is no fear of its consequences. (91:15)

[b] But he had no authority over them except that We might test the man who believe in the Hereafter from him who is in doubt concerning it --- (34:21)

[c] Amongst us (Jinns) are some that submit their wills (to God), and some that swerve from justice. Now those who submit their wills - they have sought out (the path) of right conduct: (72:14)

the Day of Judgment will be based on the choices they made in this life.^d Unfortunately Satan used his free will to defy the order of God, to insist upon his choice, and to challenge God's decision.^e As such he is destined for hell.

The Characteristic of Satan:

As his name indicates, he is disappointed (Iblees) that the human being are the Vicegeerent of God and not the Jinns. He is evil (*shaytan*), the cursed (*rajeem*), ungrateful, rebel (*aseeya*), persistent rebel (*mareeda*), chief deceiver, and the enemy of and traitor to human beings.[f]

---

[d] And to all are (assigned) degrees according to the deeds which they (have done), and in order that (God) may recompense their deeds and no injustice be done to them. (46:18-19)

If We had so willed, We could certainly have brought every soul its true guidance: But the Word from Me will come true, "I will fill Hell with Jinns (*al-jinnah*) and human being (*al-naas*) all together. (32:13)

[e] O my father! Serve not Satan, for Satan is a rebel against (God) Most Gracious. (19:44)

[f] I commend her (Maryam) and her offspring to Your protection from Satan the Rejected (*rajeem*). (3:36)

Satan is to his Lord (Himself) ungrateful. (17:27)

Satan is a rebel (*aseeya*) against (God) Most Gracious. (19:44)

They call but upon Satan, the persistent rebel (*mareeda*). (4:116)

Satan is but a traitor (*khadhoola*) to human being. (25:29)

--- and follow not the footsteps of Satan, for he is to you an open enemy. (2:168, 208, 6:142)

---- for Satan is to man an avowed enemy. (17:53, 12:5)

---- Ah! Satan is but a traitor to man. (25:29)

---- for he (Satan) is an enemy that manifestly misleads. (28:15)

Satan and the Messengers:

It is in the nature of Satan to be the staunch enemy of Prophets,[g] who are a threat to Satan's plan. One of his strategies in opposing the messengers and the prophets is to put doubts in the minds of people who listen to the message of God.[h]

O men! Certainly the promise of God is true. Let not then this present life deceive you, nor let the Chief Deceiver (Satan) deceive you about God. (35:5)

Verily Satan is an enemy to you. So treat him as an enemy. He only invites his adherents, that they may become companions of the Blazing Fire. (35:6)

Let not Satan hinder you, for he is to you an enemy avowed. (43:62)
--- Will you then take him and his progeny as protectors rather than Me. And they are enemies to you. (18:50)

[g] Likewise did We make for every Messenger an enemy - evil ones among humans (*al-ins*) and the Jinns (*al-jinn*), inspiring each other with flowery discourses by way of deception. If your Lord had so planned, they would not have done it: so leave them and their inventions alone. (6:112)

[h] Never did We send a messenger or a prophet before you (Muhammad), but, when he did recite the revelation or narrated or spoke, Satan threw (some falsehood) in it. But God abolishes that which Satan throws in. Then God establishes His revelations. And God is All-Knower, All-Wise. (22:52) NQ

When they are told to follow the (revelation) that God has sent down, they say: "Nay, we shall follow the ways the we found our fathers (following). What! Even if it is Satan beckoning them to the Penalty of the (Blazing) Fire. (31:21)

Before you We sent (messengers) to many nations, and We afflicted the nations with suffering and adversity that they might learn humility. When the suffering reached them form Us, why then did they not learn humility? On the contrary their hearts became hardened, and Satan made their (sinful) acts seem alluring to them. (6:43-44)

Basic Beliefs of Satan:
The dialogue between God and Satan (Appendix A) suggests that Satan did believe in the oneness of God and the Day of Judgement. It was his belief in the oneness of God that he swore by His power.[i] It was his belief in the Day of Judgement that he begged to live until the end of the world.[j] He also believed in the sovereignty of God and His Lordship and that is why he begged for respite from him.[k] He also fears God.[l] But he did not agree with the decision of God to make human being his vicegerent on the earth. He did not believe that human being is worthy of that status.[m]

Satan on the Day of Resurrection:
Satan, being a Jinn, is accountable for his deeds.[n] This accountability will take place on the Day of Judgment. Satan will

---

[i] --- By Your Power, I will put them all in the wrong - except Your Servants among them, sincere and purified (by Your grace). (38:82-83)

[j] He (Satan) said: "give me respite till the day they are raised up." (7:14)

(Iblis) said: "O my Lord! give me then respite till the Day the (dead) are raised." (15:36, 38:79)

[k] He (Satan) said: "give me respite till the day they are raised up." (7:14)

(Iblis) said: "O my Lord! give me then respite till the Day the (dead) are raised." (15:36, 38:79)

[l] (Their allies deceived them), like Satan when he says to man, "Deny God". But when (man) denies God, (Satan) says, "I am free of you, I do fear God the Lord of the Worlds!" (59:16)

[m] "Don't You see? This is the one whom You have honored above me! If You will but respite me to the Day of Judgment I will surely bring his descendants under my sway all but a few!" (17:62)

[n] Soon shall We settle your affairs, O both you worlds (the Jinns and the human being). (55:31)

die when the world ends. He will then be resurrected on the Day of Judgment and will be judged. On that day he will accept the falsehood of his actions.°

Summary:
Satan, like all other Jinns, was created to worship God, instead he decided to worship his pride and insisted on it. So he became the cursed one. He is disappointed, the evil (al-*shaytan*), the cursed (al-*rajeem*), ungrateful, a persistent rebel, chief deceiver, and enemy of and traitor to human being. He possesses all these characteristics because he chose to be so as a result of free will given to him by God.

Satan believes in the oneness of God, His Sovereignty, and His Lordship, and the Day of Judgment. He is also fearful of God. But he strongly disagreed with the decision of God to make human being the vicegerent of the earth and he is doing his best to prove his point. It was within the plan of God to let him make

---

And to all are (assigned) degrees according to the deeds which they (have done), and in order that (God) may recompense their deeds and no injustice be done to them. (46:19)

° And Satan will say when matter is decided: "It was God who gave you a promise of Truth. I too promised, but I failed in my promise to you. I had no authority over you except to call you, but you listen to me. Then reproach me not, but reproach your own souls. I cannot listen to your cries, nor can you listen to mine. I reject your former act in associating me with God. For wrongdoers there must be a Grievous Penalty. (14:22)

So, by your Lord without doubt, We shall gather them together, and (also) the Evil Ones (*al-shayateen*). Then shall We bring them forth on their knees round about Hell. (19:68)

The end of both will be that they will go into Fire, dwelling therein forever. Such is the reward of the wrongdoers. (59:17)

And to those straying in Evil, the Fire will be placed in full view. And it shall be said to them: "Where are the (gods) you worshipped – besides God? Can they help you or help themselves?" Then they will be thrown headlong into the (fire) – They and those straying in Evil, and the whole host of Iblees together. (26:91-95)

this decision. The plan was to distinguish those humans, who believe in the Hereafter (concept of accountability) from those who do not. He will die at the end of the world and will be resurrected and will be accountable for his deeds. He will accept the falsehood of his action and will go to hell on the Day of Judgment.

Chapter 15
The Power and Influence of Satan

Satan, as mentioned in the previous few chapters, has declared his uttermost animosity with the human being. His animosity started when God ordered all the creation to bow to Adam^{AS} (see Appendix A for detail). All complied except Satan. His pride kept him from obeying the order of God. He was proud of the fact that, whereas Adam^{AS} was created from clay, he was created from fire. In his opinion Adam^{AS} was not worthy of being His vicegerent on the earth. He challenged God that most of the human being will abandon this role.[a] God accepted his challenge and allowed him to use all the power under his disposal.[b]

---

[a] He said "Don't You see? This is the one whom You have honored above me! If You will but respite me to the Day of Judgment I will surely bring his descendants under my sway all but a few!" (17:62)

--- "I will take of Your servants a portion marked off. I will mislead them, and I will create in them false desires. I will order them to slit the ears of cattle, and to deface the (fair) nature created by God --- (4:118-119)

--- I will lie in wait for them on Your Straight Way. Then I will assault them from before them and behind them, and from their right and their left. Nor will You find, in most of them, gratitude (from Your mercies). (7:16-17)

--- I will make (wrong) fair-seeming to them on the earth. and I will put them all in the wrong, except Your servants among them, sincere and purified (by Your grace). (15:39-40)

--- By Your Power, I will put them all in the wrong - except Your Servants among them, sincere and purified (by Your grace). (38:82-83)

[b] "Lead to destruction those whom you can among them with your (seductive) voice, make assaults on them with your cavalry and your infantry, mutually share with them wealth and children and make promises to them. But Satan promises nothing but deceit. (17:64)

In order to prove his point, he asked God to let him live until the end of the world. His wish was granted. Although God has given Satan some power over the human being, He has forewarned the humans about his enmity[c] He has warned them again and again not to fall into the footsteps of Satan.[d]

Power of Satan:
As mentioned in earlier chapter, his headquarter is upon the ocean.[e] Satan, having a limited speed (about 850 miles per hour), cannot be everywhere at the same time. But he has at his disposal a huge army consisting of infantry and cavalry.[f] Among

---

[c] O you Children of Adam! Let not Satan seduce you, in the same manner as he got your parents out of the Garden, stripping them of their raiment, to expose their shame. (7:27)

Did I not enjoin on you, O you children of Adam, that you should not worship Satan, for that he was to you an enemy avowed? (36:60)

[d] O you people! Eat of what is on the earth lawful and good. And do not follow the footsteps of Satan, for he is to you an avowed enemy. (2:168)

O you who believe! Enter into Islam wholeheartedly. And follow not the footsteps of Satan, for he is to you an avowed enemy. (2:208)

Of the cattle are some for burden and some for meat. Eat what God has provided for you and follow not the footsteps of Satan, for he is to you an avowed enemy. (6:142)

O you who believe! Follow not the footsteps of Satan. If any will follow the footsteps of Satan, he will (but) command what is shameful and wrong. (24:21)

[e] The throne of Iblis is upon the ocean and he sends detachments (to different parts) in order to put people to trial and the most important figure in his eyes is one who is most notorious in sowing the seed of dissension. (Muslim:6754)

[f] "----- Lead to destruction those whom you can among them with your (seductive) voice, make assaults on them with your cavalry and your

his army are his children, his tribe, and his followers.[g] He sends his army all over the world to carry out his orders.[h] In addition, he takes the assistance of the evil Jinn attached to every human being.[i]

    Although Satan has at his disposal a host of infantry and cavalry, the only power he and his army have over the humans is the power to call and persuade.[j]

---

infantry, mutually share with them wealth and children and make promises to them. But Satan promises nothing but deceit. (17:64)

[g] Will you then take him (Satan) and his progeny (*dhurriat*) as protectors rather than Me? (18:50)

He (Satan) and his tribes watch you from a position where you cannot see them. (7:27)

--- the whisperer (of Evil), who withdraws (after his whisper) - (The same) who whispers into the hearts of Mankind – among Jinns and among Men. (114:4-6)

[h] Iblis (Satan) places his throne upon water. He then sends detachments (for creating dissension). The nearer to him in rank are those who are most notorious in creating dissension. One of them comes and says: I did so and so. And he says: You have done nothing. Then one amongst them comes and says: I did not spare so and so until I sowed the seed of discord between a husband and wife. The Satan goes near him and says: You have done well. He then embraces him. (Muslim: 6755)

[i] There is none amongst you with whom is not attached from amongst the jinn (devil). --- Yes (even with me), but God helps me against him and so I am safe from his hand and he does not command me but for good. (Muslim: 6757, 6758)

(Devil) is attached to everyone, ---- (even with me), but my Lord has helped me against him and as such I am absolutely safe from his mischief. (Muslim: 6759)

[j] And Satan will say when matter is decided: ----- I had no authority over you except to call you, but you listened to me. -----." (14:22)

They do it by feeding bad ideas to the human mind. Since they can enter the human body and run into the blood stream, they have access to the human brain and influence the thought process of the human being.[k] Satan can also influence the humans through dreams. Most of the bad dreams come from him.[l]

Satan, being one of the Jinns, can also acquire human form and talk to them face to face to do his job.

---

[k] Satan runs in the body of Adam's son (i.e. man) as his blood circulates in it, and I was afraid that he (Satan) might insert an evil thought in your hearts. (Bukhari: 8.238, 3.255)

Satan reaches everywhere in the human body as blood reaches in it, (everywhere in one's body). I was afraid lest Satan might insert an evil thought in your minds. (Bukhari: 3.251)

Satan circulates in the human being as blood circulates in the body, and I was afraid lest Satan might insert an evil thought in your minds. (Bukhari: 3.254, 4.501)

Verily Satan circulates in the body like blood. (Muslim: 5404)

Satan penetrates in man like the penetration of blood (in every part of body). (Muslim: 5405)

Verily Satan flows in the blood stream of Adam's descendent. (Sunan Abu Dawood)[1]

Verily Satan influences arteries and veins through blood. (Bukhari and Muslim)[2]

[l] A good dream that comes true is from God, and a bad dream is from Satan, so if anyone of you sees a bad dream, he should seek refuge with God from Satan and should spit on the left, for the bad dream will not harm him. (Bukhari: 9.115, 9.113, 9.124, 9.133, 9.168, 9.169, 4.513, 7.643)

Satan and his followers use their power to suggest, seduce, and persuade.[m]

Tricks of Satan:
Satan uses many tricks to achieve his objectives:

(a) He inspires greed of wealth.[n] Any moral action whether standing up for justice or helping others has its worldly consequences. The person may fear the loss of his job or his hard-earned money. It is the greed of wealth, inspired by Satan, which keeps the person from converting his conviction into action.

(b) He puts the fear of his friends.[o] Many friends of Satan have power, glory, and an abundance of wealth in this life.

---

[m] --- the whisperer (of Evil), who withdraws (after his whisper) - (The same) who whispers into the hearts of Mankind - among Jinns and among Men. (114:4-6)

Satan exercises his influence upon the son of Adam and so does the angel exercise his influence (upon him). The influence of Satan is that he holds the promise of evil and denial of truth. And the influence of the angel is that he holds the promise of good and the affirmation of truth. Thus he who perceives this (i.e. good promise) he should praise God and he who finds contrary to it, he should seek refuge with God from Satan, the accursed. He then recited this verse: `Satan threatens you with the prospect of poverty and bids you to be indecent.' (2:268) (Tirmidhi: 74)

O ye Children of Adam! Let not Satan seduce you --- (7:27)

(Iblees said:) "By Your power I will seduce all of them (human being) except Your purified servants." (38:82-83)

Then Satan began to whisper suggestion to them (Adam and his wife) in order to reveal to them their shame that was hidden from them. (7:20)

[n] Satan threatens you with poverty and bids you to conduct unseemly --- (2:268)

[o] It is only Satan that suggests to you the fear of his votaries --- (3:175)

Standing up against them may throw shiver in the hearts of well-intentioned people. Satan is the one who inculcates this fear.

(c) He sows the seed of dissension between husband and wife, brothers and sisters, friends, relatives, communities, and nations.[p] This brings conflict, war, and misery to both the parties. He sowed the seed of jealousy in the heart of Prophet Joseph's brothers, One of the tool he uses to sow dissension is the promotion of gambling, alcohol, and drugs.[q]

---

[p] --- Satan does sow dissension among them (human being). (17:53)

My dear little son (Yousuf)! Relate not your vision (dream) to your brothers, lest they concoct a plot against you. For Satan is to man an avowed enemy. (12:5)

O my father (Yaqoob)! This is the fulfillment of my vision of old! God has made it come true! He was indeed good to me when He took me out of prison and brought you (all here) out of the desert, (even) after Satan had sown enmity between me and my brothers. (12:100)

The throne of Iblis is upon the ocean and he sends detachments (to different parts) in order to put people to trial and the most important figure in his eyes is one who is most notorious in sowing the seed of dissension. (Muslim: 6754)

Iblis places his throne upon water. He then sends detachments (for creating dissension). The nearer to him in rank are those who are most notorious in creating dissension. One of them comes and says: I did so and so. And he says: You have done nothing. Then one amongst them comes and says: I did not spare so and so until I sowed the seed of discord between a husband and wife. The Satan goes near him and says: You have done well. He then embraces him. (Muslim: 6755)

[q] Satan's plan is (but) to excite enmity and hatred between you, with intoxicants and gambling, and hinder you from the remembrance of God, and from prayer. (5:91)

(d) Painting a beautiful picture of shameful and wrong things.[r] Any shameful act is deplorable in its true form, but Satan does a good job of packaging it in such a manner that it looks beautiful. Promotion of nudity and vulgarity in the media is an excellent example of packaging shameful acts in alluring form. Nobody likes bad things done to him or her, but they do not mind doing the same to others. A robber does not like to be robbed by others, but he has no qualms about robing others, People, who create anarchy to gain power, insist on maintaining law and order once they gain power. A person, who molests others, would fight back if someone does the same to him. Even intelligent and skillful people can fall into his trap.[s]

(e) He gives false hopes and creates false desires.[t] The story of Prophet Yousuf[AS] and his brothers is a good example of

---

[r] (Iblees said:) "--- I will make (wrong) fair-seeming to them (human being) on the earth, and I will put them all in the wrong. Except Your servants among them, sincere and purified (by Your Grace). (15:39-40)

Satan made their (sinful) acts seem alluring to them. (8:48, 6:43)

but Satan made (to the wicked), their own acts seem alluring --- (16:63)

Satan ---- bids you to conduct unseemly --- (2:268)

If any will follow the footsteps of Satan, he will (but) command what is shameful and wrong. (24:(21)

I found her (Queen of Saba) people worshipping the sun besides God. Satan has made their deeds seem pleasing to their eyes, and has kept them away from the Path – so they receive no guidance. (27:24)

[s] Satan made (Ad and Thamood) their deeds alluring to them, and kept them from the path, though they were gifted with intelligence and skill. (29:38)

[t] Satan makes them promises and creates in them false desires --- (4:120)

Those who turn back as apostate after Guidance was clearly shown to them – Satan has instigated them and buoyed them up with false hope. (47:25)

how Satan created false desires among his brothers. They thought that by getting rid of Yousuf[AS], they would get more love and attention from Yaqoob[AS].[u]

(f) He makes us forget the good things.[v] Every now and then we get good ideas, or get an urge to do something good, but if we do not follow it through, we forget about it. Even if we do not forget it, we start seeing all the obstacles in the way. Both of these are from Satan or his agents.

Satan promises to them nothing but deceit. (17:64)

[u] They said: "Truly Yousuf and his brother (Bin Yameen) are loved more by our father (Yaqoob) than we. But we are goodly body. Really our father is obviously wandering (in his mind). Slay Yousuf or cast him out to some (unknown) land, that so the favor of your father may be given to you alone. (There will be time enough) for you to be righteous after that. (12:8-9)

[v] We had already, beforehand, taken the covenant of Adam, but he forgot and We found on his part no resolve. (20:115)
When you see men engaged in vain discourse about Our signs, turn away from them unless they turn to a different theme. If Satan ever makes you forget, then after recollection, sit not you in the company of those who do wrong. (6:68)

And of the two (prisoners in the jail), to that one whom he considered about to be saved (to be set free), he (Yousuf) said: "Mention me to your lord." But Satan made him forget to mention him to his lord. (12:42)

He (Moses' companion) replied: "Saw you (what happened) when we betook ourselves to the rock? I did indeed forget (about) the fish. None but Satan made me forget to tell (you) about it. It took its course through the sea in a marvelous way!" (18:63)

Satan has got the better of them so he has made them lose the remembrance of God. They are the Party of Satan. It is the Party of Satan that will perish. (58:19)

(g) He inspires secret counsel to promote iniquity and hostility.[w] Most of the conspiracies are hatched in secret. The coup de tat to topple democratically elected regimes happens in the middle of the night. Most of the crimes are committed in the dark alleys. Backbiting is always done in the absence of the person to sway other against him. Any sexual indulgence outside matrimony is immoral. All these acts are inspired by Satan. When an adult male and female are alone, Satan inspires them to indulge in immoral acts.[4]

(h) He misleads by playing with our instincts.[x] We, being a part of animal kingdom, are in many cases driven by instincts. It is our conscience that keeps a leash on our instincts. But every now and then we turn the leash loose. Satan makes the best use of those moments. Those who keep God in remembrance regret those moments and seek forgiveness. It was probably the natural instinct that caused Prophet Moses (Moosa[AS]) to punch the guy which caused his death. Prophet Moses (Moosa[AS]) had no intention of killing the guy. Unfortunately, the punch landed in the wrong place. He immediately realized that Satan had played on his instincts.

---

[w] O you who believe! When you hold secret counsel, do it not for iniquity, and hostility, and disobedience to the messenger; but do it for righteousness and self- restraint and fear God, to whom you shall be brought back. (58:9)

Secret counsels are only (inspired) by Satan in order that he may cause grief to the believers. But he cannot harm them in the least, except as God permits and on God let the believers put their trust. (58:10)

[x] And he (Moosa) entered the City at a time when its people were not watching and he found two men fighting – one of his own people, and the other, of his foes. Now the man of his own people appealed to him against his foe, and Moses (Moosa) struck him with his fist and made an end of him. He said: "This is a work of Satan for he is an enemy that manifestly misleads. (28:15)

--- Satan's wish is to lead them (human being) astray, far away (from the Right). (4:60)

Victims of Satan:
God has not only warned the human being about the enmity of Satan, He has also warned them the kind of behavior that will cause them to loose the battle against Satan. The following are some of those characteristics:

(a) Those who withdraw themselves from the remembrance of God.[y] Space is never unoccupied. If it has nothing, it has air to fill in. So is the heart of humans. If it does not have the remembrance of God, it has Satan in it. Those who give up the remembrance of God, are making room for Satan in their heart. Satan then becomes their friend and motivates them to do evil acts.

(b) Those who do not put their trust in God.[z] Life is full of ups and down. If we lose faith and trust in God during the down phase of life, we may adopt the ways of Satan to overcome this phase. We know stealing is not good, but it requires extra effort to not to resort to stealing when someone is out of job and has few hungry children to feed.

---

[y] If anyone withdraws himself from remembrance of (God) Most Gracious, We appoint for him an evil one (satan), to be an intimate companion to him. Such (evil one) really hinder them from the Path. but they think that they are being guided aright. At length, when (such a one) comes to Us, he says (to his evil companion): "Would that between me and you were the distance of East and West" Ah! evil is the companion (indeed). (43:36-38)

Every human being has two houses in his heart. In one house lives an angel and in the other house lives satan (evil Jinn). The angel persuades him to do good deeds and the satan persuades him to do bad deeds. When he is busy remembering God, the satan backs off. When he is not busy in remembrance of God, the satan persuades him to do bad deeds.[3] (Prophet Muhammad[SAW])

[z] No authority has he (Satan) over those who believe and put their trust in their Lord. (16:99)

(c) Those who take Satan as patron and join partners with God.[aa] As mentioned earlier, those who give up the remembrance of God, make room for Satan in their heart. Satan then becomes their patron and drives their actions.

(d) Our actions can make us vulnerable to Satan, [ab] for example, those who practice lying and wickedness. People who have no faith and trust in God want to have their way quick and without much effort usually resort to lying and wickedness. They do get ahead in life in the short run and believe that their methodology is good. It is Satan who paints this rosy picture. They get deeper and deeper in their crime.

Friends of Satan:
Adoption of certain behavior and attitude gets him closer to Satan and away from God. The following are some of the behaviors and attitude, which makes a person a friend of Satan:

(a) Those who have no faith in God and the Day of Judgment.[ac] As mentioned earlier, people who lose faith in God

---

[aa] His (Satan's) authority is over those only who take him as patron and who join partners with God. (16:100)

God is the Protector of those who have faith: from the depths of darkness He will lead them forth into light. Of those who reject faith the patrons are the Evil Ones: from light they will lead them forth into the depths of darkness. They will be companions of the fire to dwell therein (for ever). (2:257)

[ab] Those of you who turned back on the day the two host met (Battle of Uhd), -- it was Satan who caused them to fail, because of some (evil) they had done. (3:155)

Shall I inform you, (O people) on whom it is that Satan descend? They descend on every lying, wicked person. (Into whose ears) they pour hearsay vanities and most of them are liars. 26 (221-223)

But Satan made (to the wicked), their own acts seem alluring --- (16:63)

[ac] Whoever, forsaking God, takes Satan for a friend, has of a surety suffered a loss that is manifest. (4:119)

give Satan a residence in their heart. He then becomes their best friend. Those who lose faith in God also do not believe in the accountability of their actions on the Day of Judgement. They then become shortsighted and look for quick return for their actions in this life. We all know that long term investment brings more profit than short term investment. But it requires sticking with the course of action for the long haul.

(b) Those who blindly follow their forefathers (or culture).[ad] It is true that culture is the best way to maintain stability in a society. But it requires constant rejuvenation to remain dynamic. It must go through a constant scrutiny to keep the good and trash out the bad. This runs contrary to interest of Satan. People who oppose the scrutiny of culture thus become a friend of Satan.

(c) Those who ignore the signs of God and do not take lessons from events happening around them.[ae] Humans are by nature forgetful. They need a constant reminder to stay the course of the ways of God. God has designed the world in a way

---

Nor those who spend of their substance, to be seen of men, but have no faith in God and the Last Day. If any takes Satan for their intimate, what a dreadful intimate he is! (4:38)

Of those who reject faith the patrons are the Evil Ones (Taghoot). From light they will lead them forth into depth of darkness. They will be companions of the fire, to dwell therein (forever). (2:257)

And yet among men there are such as dispute about God, without knowledge, and follow every evil one obstinate in rebellion! (22:4)

See you not that We have Satan on against unbelievers to incite them with furry. (19:83)

[ad] When they are told to follow the (revelation) that God has sent down, they say: "Nay, we shall follow the ways we found our fathers (following). What! Even if it is Satan beckoning them to the Penalty of the (Blazing) Fire. (31:21)

[ae] Relate to them the story of the man whom We sent Our Signs, but he passed them by. So Satan followed him up, and he went astray. (7:175)

that constantly exposes humans to signs that reminds them of his purpose in life. People who ignore these signs forget the purpose of life. They wander aimlessly in life under the friendship of Satan.

(d) Those who squander or waste resources put at their disposal. This could be time, talent, material possessions, and etc.[af] We are as much vulnerable in prosperity to the trick of Satan as in adversity. Whereas adversity requires patience to stay with God, prosperity requires self control in prosperity. Becoming wasteful in such situation opens the door of friendship with Satan. He then persuades the person to waste his resources in non-productive or useless things and activities.

(e) Those who do charity to show off.[ag] People who do things to show off are oblivious to the accountability of the Day of Judgement. Satan loves those who do not care about this accountability and becomes their best friend.

Whoever is a friend of Satan is doomed[ah] and becomes the worst of the creatures.[ai] They help each other in their rebellion against God.[aj]

[af] Verily spendthrifts are brothers of Satan and Satan is to his Lord (Himself) ungrateful. (17:27)

About (Satan) it is decreed that whoever turns to him for friendship, him will he lead astray. And he will guide him to the penalty of the Fire. (22:4)

[ag] Nor those who spend of their substance, to be seen of men, but have no faith in God and the Last Day. If any takes Satan for their intimate, what a dreadful intimate he is! (4:38)

[ah] If any takes Satan for their intimate, what a dreadful intimate he is! (4:38)

Satan has got the better of them. So he has made them lose the remembrance of God. They are the party of Satan. Truly it is the party of Satan that will perish. (58:19)

[ai] Then do We abase him (to be) the lowest of the low. (95:5)

Instead of worshipping and serving God, they start worshipping Satan and other evil Jinns.[ak] They do not even hesitate to invent blood relationship between the Jinns and God.[al] Instead of taking protection with God, they take shelter with Satan and evil Jinns.[am]

[aj] One day will He gather them all together, (and say): "O you assembly of Jinns (*al-jinn*)! Much (toll) did you take of men (*al-ins*)." Their friends amongst men will say: "Our Lord! we made profit from each other; but (alas!) we reached our term - which You did appoint for us." He will say: "The Fire be your dwelling therein forever, except as God wills, for your Lord is full of wisdom and knowledge.(6:128)

[ak] (Ibraheem said:) "O my father! Serve not Satan! for Satan is a rebel against (God) Most Gracious. (19:44)

One Day He will gather them al together, and say to the angels, "Was it you that these Men used to worship?" They will say, "Glory to You! Our (tie) is with You - as Protector - not with them. Nay, but they worshipped the Jinns (al-jinn): most of them believed in them. (34:40-41)

Yet they make the Jinns (*al-jinn*) equal with God, though God did create the Jinns; and they falsely, having no knowledge, attribute to Him sons and daughters. Praise and glory be to Him! (for He is) above what they attribute to Him! (6:100)

[al] And they have invented a blood relationship between Him and the Jinns (*al-jinnah*): but the Jinns (*al-jinnah*) know (quite well) that they have indeed to appear (before His Judgment Seat)! Glory to God! (he is free) from the things they ascribe (to Him). (37:158-159)

[am] Behold! we said to the angels, "Bow down to Adam": they bowed down except Iblees. He was one of the Jinns (*al-jinn*), and he broke the Command of his Lord. Will you then take him and his progeny (*dhurriat*) as protectors rather than Me? And they are enemies to you! Evil would be the exchange for the wrongdoers. (18:50)

True, there were persons (*rijaal*) among mankind (al-ins) who took shelter with persons (rijaal) among the jinns (*al-jinn*), but they increased them in folly. (72:6)

The Touch of Satan:

We are swimming in the sea of air. As we move around we are constantly being brushed with air. Since Satan or his agent Jinns are made from carbon dioxide, we cannot avoid being touched by him or his agents if they desire to do so.

Mental Ailment or Being Possessed

A touch by Satan can cause mental ailment, as it will happen to people who devour usury.[an] The brain activity is a very complex psychological phenomenon and requires a delicate electrical and chemical balance. We know that a sudden financial or emotional disaster or shock sometimes causes heart attacks or mental instability. People who are familiar with the Holy Quran know that emotional and financial loses are test of God.[ao] So good people remain calm when they suffer any calamity. People, who give up the remembrance of God, become materialistic and are mentally (psychologically) unprepared to handle calamities.[ap]

[an] Those who devour usury will not stand except as stands one whom Satan by his touch has driven to madness. This is because they say: "Trade is like usury." (2:275)

[ao] O You who believe! Seek help with patient Perseverance and Prayer, for God is with those who patiently persevere. -----. Be sure We shall test you with something of fear and hunger, some loss in goods or lives or fruits (of your toil). Give glad tidings to those who patiently persevere - who say, when afflicted with calamity: "To God we belong, and to Him is our return." They are those on whom (descends) blessings from their Lord, and Mercy, and they are the ones who receive guidance. (2:153, 155-157)

[ap] Man does not weary of asking for good (things), but if ill touches him, he gives up all hope (and) is lost in despair. (41:49)

If We give man a taste of mercy from Ourselves, and then withdraw it form him, behold! He is in despair and (falls into) blasphemy. But if We give him a taste of (Our) favors after adversity has touched him, he is sure to say, "All evil has departed form me." Behold! He falls into exultation and pride. Not so do those who show patience and constancy, and work righteousness. (11:9-11)

Since Satan has access to the brain, he may disturb the electrical and chemical balance in the brain of those who give up the remembrance of God, causing them to go crazy.

Physical Ailments

A touch by Satan can also cause disease, as it happened to Prophet Job (Ayoob[AS]).[aq] He was covered with sores from head to toe, which he attributed to the touch of Satan. Since Satan can penetrate the human body, he may be able to affect the chemical balance in the blood or the body to cause sores or other ailments.

The distress in life is also a test. It is a test of our patience and a test of whom do we turn to under distress. Those who do not put their trust in God seek refuge with the Jinns and Satan.[ar] The response of Prophet Job (Ayoob[AS]) is a shining example of the power of patience. He patiently bore his distress, put his trust in God and only took refuge with him. Most of the scholars[8] have, however, interpreted this verse to mean that "the affliction of the severities of illness, the loss of property and wealth, and the desertion of the near ones and dear ones, is not so great a torment and trouble for me as the temptation of Satan, who is exploiting my condition to despair me of my Lord and wants that I should turn ungrateful to Him and become desperate and impatient."

When trouble touches a man, he cries unto Us (in all postures) – lying down, on his side, or sitting, or standing. But when We have solved his trouble, he passes on his way as if he had never cried to Us for a trouble that touched him! (10:11)

[aq] Commemorate Our Servant Job (Ayoob). Behold he cried to his Lord: "Satan has afflicted (touched) with distress and suffering! (38:41)

And (remember) Job (Ayoob), when he cried to his Lord, "Truly distress has seized (touched) me. But You are the Most Merciful of those that are Merciful." (21:83)

[ar] True, there were persons among mankind who took shelter with persons among Jinns, but they increased them in folly. (72:6)

If any take Satan for their intimate, what a dreadful intimate he is! (4:38)

Protection from Satan:

Although Satan is the declared enemy of the human being and is constantly at war with him, his power is not as strong as it looks.[as] It is the human being who by letting his guards down succumbs to Satan's tricks. Once a person stops remembering God, he stops putting his full trust in Him. He, then, starts seeking other patrons for his needs. Since Satan is skillful in making evil look attractive, he (the person) starts thinking that his new patrons are the sole authority in fulfilling his needs. He then starts thinking that they are as powerful as God. He thus indulges in making partners with God. By avoiding the behaviors mentioned above, he can avoid losing the battle against Satan.

There are many situations in which the human being can protect himself from the attacks of Satan by seeking refuge with God and are given below.

Bad thoughts

As mentioned earlier, Satan is usually the instigator of bad thoughts in the human being. In such situations the Holy Quran advises us to "seek refuge with God from Satan, the Cursed."[at]

When Abused by Others

Not all humans are alike. Some are good and some are bad. Sometimes we may find ourselves in a situation where we may feel as if we are being verbally or physically abused. In such a situation, we may be tempted to do the same to others. The Holy Quran, however, advises us to seek refuge with God not only from the suggestions of the evil ones, but also that they should come near him.[au]

[as] --- feeble indeed is the cunning of Satan. (4: 76)

[at] If a suggestion from Satan assails your (mind), seek refuge with God, for He hears and knows (all things). Those who fear God, when a thought of evil from Satan assaults them, bring God to remembrance, when lo! They see (aright). (7: 200-201)

[au] Repel evil with that which is best. We are well acquainted with the things they say. And say "O my Lord! I seek refuge with You from the suggestions of the evil ones (*al-shayateen*). And I seek refuge with You O my Lord! lest they should come near me. (23:96-98)

When Angry
The vulnerability to the attack of Satan increases during anger. The Holy Quran and Prophet Muhammad[SAW] have advised us that in such situations we should seek refuge with God from Satan, the Cursed.[av]

When Reading Quran
Depending upon our attitude with which we approach the Holy Quran, it could guide us or misguide us. We should approach the Holy Quran for the sake of seeking guidance. As such we should drive out bad thoughts before approaching the Holy Quran. Since Satan is the instigator of bad thought, we should seek refuge with God from Satan, the Cursed before reciting the Holy Book.[aw]

Why God Permitted Satan?:
It may look puzzling why God allowed Satan to persuade the humans to do shameful and wrong things. As has been mentioned earlier, the very reason for creating the human being and the Jinns was that they would willingly serve God.[ax] This sense of responsibility will only come when a person strongly believes in the concept of accountability. The purpose for allowing Satan was to distinguish those who believe in the Hereafter (concept of accountability) from those who are not sure about it.[ay]

[av] Repel evil with that which is best. Then will he between whom and you was hatred become as it were your friend and intimate. ----- And if (at any time) an incitement to discord is made to you by Satan seek refuge in God, He is the One who hears and knows all things. (41:34, 36)

[aw] When you read the Quran, seek God's protection from Satan, the Rejected One. No authority has he (Satan) over those who believe and put their trust in their Lord. (16: 98-99)

[ax] I have only created Jinns and human being, that they will serve Me. (51: 56)

[ay] But he had no authority over them except that We might test the man who believe in the Hereafter from him who is in doubt concerning it --- (34: 21)

Summary

Satan is the declared enemy of the human being. His animosity started when God asked him, all creatures included, to bow to Adam^{AS}. He refused to accept the superiority of the human being. He challenged God that the human being does not deserve such a status. He claimed that he could prove his point if he is allowed to live until the end of the world. God granted him his wish. God has, however, forewarned the human being about his enmity and not to fall in his footsteps. The wisdom behind granting him his wish was to distinguish those who believe in the Hereafter from those who do not.

The only power Satan has over the human being is to plant evil ideas in his mind. He uses this power to persuade and seduce him. He has at his disposal a huge army, which includes his progeny, his tribe, and his follower Jinns. They go around the world to implement his orders. He is also helped by the evil Jinns attached with every human being. He (and his army) feed bad ideas to our mind when we are awake as well as when we are asleep (in the form of bad dreams). He uses many tricks to achieve his objective. He inspires greed of wealth, fear of his votaries, sows seeds of dissension among people, paints beautiful picture of shameful and wrong things, gives false hopes, creates false desires, makes us forget good things, inspires secret counsel to promote iniquity and hostility, and misleads us.

Satan can also affect the human being by his touch. His touch can cause mental illness, but this can only happen to people who have not mentally prepared themselves for the calamities they may face as a part of the test of this life. His touch may also cause disease, which is also a test of this life as it happened with Prophet Job (Ayoob^{AS}).

His power and tricks are not as strong as it seems. However, those who give up the remembrance of God, do not put their trust in Him, take Satan as their patron, join partners with God, and practice lying and cheating become his victims. The Holy Quran has also defined certain characteristics that make a person a friend of Satan. This includes those who reject God, the Day of Judgment, and His signs, those who squander resources, and those who do charity to show off. They end up worshipping Satan and taking protection with him. The human being can protect himself from Satan's attack and tricks by taking protection with God.

Chapter 16
Summary

Satan is an Islamic-Judeo-Christian term that stands for the Devil. He is a being who is the instigator of all the evil acts. The Arabic equivalent of Satan is '*al-shaytan*, pronounced as '*ash-shaytan*'. In the Holy Quran, the term *al-shaytan* is used for a particular being who refused to bow to Adam^{AS}, when he was ordered to do so by God. The proper name of that particular being is Iblees. The literal meaning of Iblees is the one who is disappointed. He is given the title of Satan for his evil characteristics.

Satan, according to the Holy Quran, belongs to the class of the Jinns. Being one of the Jinns, Satan should also be of gaseous origin. His gaseous nature makes him invisible, imperceptible, and penetrable. It gives him great power and flexibility in size and shape. He can travel at an average speed of about 850 miles per hour, and can fathom space up to an altitude of about 60 to 70 miles. Probably due to his flexibility in size and shape, he can also acquire human and animal forms. The human being does not possess these characteristics. This is due to the difference in the origin of the two, but both inhabit the planet earth. Whereas most of the human beings live on the continents, Satan has made his headquarter upon the ocean.

Satan has many of the same biological characteristics found in the human being and other animals of cellular origin. He has female companion and replicates to produce children, and will die at the end of the world. He consumes food to generate energy and maintain his health. Satan, like the human being, has the power of observation and intelligence. He communicates with humans through their thought process. He may also converse directly with them after acquiring human form. He can also listen to the conversation of the angels, if it is carried out within an altitude of about 70 miles. He also conversed with God at the time of creation of Adam^{AS}. The ordinary human being, however, cannot communicate with Satan or transform into other beings.

Satan and the Jinns, though created before the humans, are, however, inferior to him. Though Satan and the Jinns had the advantage over the human being in power, speed, and space travel at the time of the creation of Adam^{AS}, the humans have surpassed them by technological innovation.

Satan, like all the other Jinns, was created to worship God. He believed in the oneness of God, His Sovereignty, and His Lordship, and the Day of Judgment. But upon the creation of Adam^{AS}, he refused to bow to him. At that moment he chose to follow his pride instead of following the order of God. He thus became the cursed one, the evil (*al-shaytan*), and the rejected (*al-rajeem*). He will die at the end of the world, will be resurrected on the Day of Judgment, and will be accountable for his deeds. He will accept the falsehood of his actions and will go to hell.

Satan is an enemy of the human being. However, the only power he has over the humans is to give him bad ideas. He uses this power to persuade and seduce. He has at his disposal a huge army, which include his progeny, his tribe, and his follower Jinns. They go around the world to implement his orders. He is also helped by the evil Jinn attached with every human being. He and his troops feed bad ideas to the human mind whether he is awake or asleep (in the form of bad dreams). He uses many tricks to achieve his objective. He inspires greed of wealth, fear of his friends, sows seeds of dissension among people, paints beautiful picture of shameful and wrong things, gives false hopes, creates false desires, makes us forget good things, inspires secret counsel to promote iniquity and hostility, and misleads us. His power and tricks, however, are not as strong as it seems. Only those who give up the remembrance of God become his victims. They end up worshipping Satan and taking protection with him. The human being can protect himself from Satan's attack and tricks by taking protection with God.

SECTION III

ANGELS

Chapter 17
The Origin of the Angels

The Holy Quran does not make any direct statement about the origin of the angels. However, it does talk about their speed.[a] The Holy Quran states that the angels and the Spirit (*Ar-Rooh*) ascend to God at a speed such that their day is equal to fifty thousand years of ours. Most of the scholars [1,2,3] have interpreted '*Ar-Rooh*' and '*Rooh*' for Angel Gabriel (Jibraeel[AS]).

The Speed of Ascension of the Angels:
The Quranic statements suggest that time is not an absolute quantity.[b] Einstein, in his theory of relativity, also showed that both time and distance are not absolute.[4] The two depend upon the speed with which the object is moving relative to each other.[c] Time slows down as the speed increases and becomes standstill at the speed of light, which is 670 million miles per hour (186,000 miles per second). This effect is called time dilation.[5] According to this theory, thousand years of ours at rest will be equal to a day at the speed of 669,999,999.997 miles per hour. The speed at which one day corresponds to 50,000 years of ours

---

[a] The angels and the Spirit (*Ar-Rooh*) ascend unto Him in a Day the measure whereof is (as) fifty thousand years. (70:4)

[b] Verily a day in the sight of your Lord is like a thousand years of your reckoning. (22:47)

He rules (all) affairs from the heavens to the earth: in the end will (all affairs) go (*raja'*) up to Him on a Day the space whereof will be (as) a thousand years of your reckoning. (32:5)

[c] The ratio of the time elapsed on the watch of a moving object to the time elapsed on the watch of a stationary object is given by:
$$[1 - (\text{speed of the moving object} / \text{the speed of light})^2]^{0.5}$$

is 669,999,999.999999 miles per hour. Thus for all practical purpose a day at the speed of light is more than thousand years of ours. The Holy Quran, in view of current understanding of science, is suggesting that the speed of the angels is the speed of light.

The Basic Constituent of the Angels:
According to Einstein's famous energy equation[d], it is impossible for a particle of any mass to reach the speed of light.[6] Only a particle of zero mass can reach the speed of light.[7] Thus compared to the humans, who are made from cells that possess mass, the angels are made from particles that have zero mass.

The statement of Prophet Muhammad[SAW] suggests that the angels are made from light.[e] A light beam, according to Einstein, consists of a stream of tiny packets of energy called photons.[8] According to this theory, a source of light is in effect shoots a stream of photons. A typical one-hundred-watt bulb emits about a hundred billion billion (10^{20}) photons per second. The energy of photon depends upon the frequency of the light wave it comprises. Higher the frequency of the wave, higher is the energy of the photon comprising the wave.[9] The light beam upon interaction with the retina gives us the sensation of sight.[10] It is composed of seven colors: violet, indigo, blue, green, orange, yellow, and red. The highest frequency of the visible light corresponds to violet color and lowest frequency corresponds to red color.

Thus in view of the Quranic statement, the statement of Prophet Muhammad[SAW], and our current understanding of science, we will propose that the angels are made from tiny packets of energy called photon, which has the following characteristics:

---

[d] Energy = Mass x Velocity of Light^2 or [$E = mc^2$]

[e] God's Apostle (peace be upon him) said: The Angels were born out of light and the Jinns were born out of the spark of fire and Adam was born as he has been defined (in the Qur'an) for you (i.e. he is fashioned out of clay). (Muslim: 7134)

it has no mass;
it travels at the speed of light; and
it has energy corresponding to the frequency of the wave it comprises.

Photon, according to Physics, is a force particle and is associated with electromagnetic force.[11] It is the electromagnetic force that carries the photons. We will propose that the angels could be behind the electromagnetic force or may in fact be the force themselves. Electromagnetic force is responsible for keeping electrons in orbit around the nucleus. It is ultimately responsible for the existence of atoms and molecules, and hence is the basis of life. It holds our bones and skins together. In modern life, the electromagnetic force is also responsible for driving lights, computers, radio, telephones, television, many kitchen appliances, and many other conveniences.

Types of Angels:
The Holy Quran tells us that angels have two, three, and four pairs of wings.[f] The wings stand for the power of angels. The statements of Prophet Muhammad[SAW] suggests[12,13] that their wings are not limited to four.[g] On two occasions, Prophet Muhammad[SAW] saw Angel Gabriel with six hundred wings. The first vision took place when Prophet Muhammad[SAW] received the first revelation at Jabl-Noor.[h] The second vision[i] took place when

---

[f] Praise be to God Who created (out of nothing) the heavens and the earth Who made the angels messengers with wings two or three or four (Pairs): He adds to Creation as He pleases: for God has power over all things. (35:1)

[g] Prophet Muhammad once saw the Angel Gabriel (Jibraeel[AS]) with six hundred wings. (Bukhari, Muslim, Tirmidhi)[14]

Prophet Muhammad had seen Angel Gabriel (Jibraeel[AS]) twice in his real shape: he had six hundred wings and had covered the whole horizon. (Tirmidhi)[15]

[h] It is no less than inspiration sent down to him: He was taught by one mighty in Power (Jibraeel), endued with Wisdom: For he appeared (in

Prophet Muhammad[SAW] went on Mi'raj (Ascension).[16] The Holy Quran calls Angel Gabriel (Jibraeel[AS]) the one mighty in power.[j] Assuming that he is the mightiest one, the wings of the angels could range from two to six hundred. Scholars have also taken wings to mean power or quality.[17,18]

We stated earlier that the angels are made from tiny mass-less packets of energy called photons, which travel at the speed of light. The photons are not only the constituent of visible light, but also of many other waves. The waves having frequencies higher than that of violet and lower than that of red are not visible to human eye. All of these waves formed by photons are called electromagnetic waves (See Appendix B for detail). Many of these waves play a significant role in modern day communication and are used in electronic appliances, diagnosis, and treatment. For example, radio waves are used for communication in radio, television, and cordless and cellular phones. Microwaves are used in microwave oven, in radar system for aircraft navigation, and for studying atomic and molecular properties of matter. Infrared waves are used in physical therapy, infrared photography, and the study of the vibrations of atoms. X-rays are used as a diagnostic tool in medicine and as a treatment for certain form of cancer. Each of

---

stately form), while he was in the highest part of the horizon: Then he approached and came closer and was at a distance of but two bow-lengths or (even) nearer.

So did (God) convey the inspiration to His Servant (conveyed) what He (meant) to convey. The (Prophet's) (mind and) heart in no way falsified that which he saw. Will you then dispute with him concerning what he saw?

[i] For indeed he saw him at a second descent. Near the Lote-tree beyond which none may pass: Near it is the Garden of Abode. Behold the Lote-tree was shrouded (in mystery unspeakable!). (His) sight never swerved nor did it go wrong! For truly did he see of the Signs of his Lord the Greatest! (53:4-18)

[j] Verily this is the word of a most honorable Messenger, endued with Power with rank before the Lord of the Throne. With authority there, (and) faithful to his trust. (81:19-21)

these waves has a particular frequency. Frequencies higher than that of violet correspond to ultraviolet ray, X-rays, gamma rays, and cosmic rays and lower. Frequencies lower than those of red correspond to infrared ray, microwaves, and radio waves.[19] Cosmic rays have the highest frequency and Radio waves have the lowest frequency.[20] The characteristics of these waves are described in Appendix B.

Since photons could have energies ranging from that of radio waves to that of cosmic rays, the angels could also have the same range of energy and power. Thus angels made from photons corresponding to Cosmic rays will be most powerful and the angels made from photons corresponding to Radio waves will be the least powerful among all the angels. According to Prophet Muhammad[SAW] the whole space in the Universe is filled with the angels. According to physicists and astronomers,[21] the universe is filled with microwave radiation. In every cubic meters of the universe there are, on average, about 400 million photons. A percentage of the "snow" we see on the television screen when the station sign off is due to this electromagnetic radiation. The angels are probably made from photons that include not only light but also other electromagnetic radiation.[k]

We have limited our discussion to photons and electromagnetic forces, but a case has been made in Appendix C that the angels could also be behind nuclear forces and gravitational forces, which are composed of gluons and gravitons, respectively.

Summary:
The analysis of the Quranic statements and the statements of Prophet Muhammad[SAW] suggests that the angels are made from photons, which have zero mass, travel at the speed of light, and possess energy corresponding to the frequency of the wave they comprise. They are probably behind the electromagnetic force or

---

[k] I see that which you do not. The Heaven cries (on account of the heavy load of the angels prostrating) and is justified in doing so. There is not a space equal to four fingers in it but is occupied by angels who are prostrating before God. Transmitted by Tirmidhi. (Al-Tirmidhi 406)

could be the force itself. This view is supported by the role played by electromagnetic force in modern day communication equipment and electronic gadgets, which basically involve communication and execution of command.

There are many types of angels, each type has a particular power. The power of these angels depends upon the frequency of the electromagnetic force their photon is part of. The angels made from photons corresponding to Cosmic rays will be the most powerful and the angels made from photons corresponding to Radio waves will be the least powerful among all the angels.

Chapter 18
The Physical Characteristics of the Angels

The physical characteristics of an object depend upon the physical characteristics of the basic building block of that object. For example, the physical characteristics of a block of iron are determined by the physical characteristics of iron particle. Since human being is comprised of cells, his physical characteristic is dictated by the physical characteristic of the cell. He is neither stiff like iron, nor fluid like water. Logic suggests that the physical characteristics of the angels, being made from photons, will be dictated by the physical characteristics of photons, which have the following characteristics:

>they have no mass;
>they travel at the speed of light;
>they have energy corresponding to the frequency of the wave it comprises.

Size and Shape:
Since stream of photons form electromagnetic waves, the physical characteristics of the angels will be similar to that of electromagnetic waves. The shape of the angels will be that of a wave. Their size will depend upon the frequency of the wave.[a]

---

[a] Frequency of electromagnetic wave = Energy of photon / Planck's Constant[8]
 (Planck's Constant = 6.63×10^{-34} Joules.second or 6.63×10^{-27} erg. second)

Wavelength = Speed of Light / Frequency of the Wave[9]
e.g. a radio wave with a frequency of 5 Mega Hertz will have a wavelength of 3×10^8 meter per second / 5×10^6 per second or 60 meter

Power = Energy / time[10]

For example, long-wave (100 kilohertz) is one million trillion (10^{18}) times bigger than cosmic rays (10^{20} kilohertz)

Energy:
Since the angels are made from photons, the angels will also possess energy. Their energy will depend upon the frequency of electromagnetic wave their photons belong to. As mentioned in the previous chapter, there are many types of electromagnetic waves, each possessing a particular amount of energy. The energy of the electromagnetic wave ranges from 4×10^{8} electron volts to 4×10^{-17} electron volts and so would be the range of energy of the angels.

Power:
Power is defined as the time rate of energy transfer.[a] Since the angels possess energy, they will also possess power, which will also be a function of the frequency of the wave their photon is associated with.

Pattern of Movement:
The Holy Quran states that the angels glide or swim (*sabaha*) in the heavens.[a] The Holy Quran has used the term '*sabaha*' for the motion of the celestial bodies in the heaven.[b] The angels float freely without any support in the heaven. The statement of Prophet Muhammad[SAW] also supports this view.[c]

---

[a] And by those who glide along (on errands of mercy) (79:3)

[b] All (the celestial bodies) swim along, each in its rounded course. (21:33)

[c] God (glorified and exalted be He) has supernumerary angels who rove about seeking out gatherings in which God's name is being invoked: they sit with them and fold their wings round each other, filling that which is between them and between the lowest heaven. When [the people in the gathering] depart, [the angels] ascend and rise up to heaven. (Hadeeth Qudsi 14)

Humans need a flat surface to move forward. Sound and water waves need air and water, respectively, as medium to travel. Light or other electromagnetic waves travel in a straight line in the form of wave.[1] These waves do not need any medium to travel. In other words, whereas humans and sound and water waves need something to move, electromagnetic waves move without any support. The angels, being made from photons, should thus glide throughout the heaven in the form of wave. They should be able to travel in a straight line without any support in a manner similar to the way light travels.

Speed:
We have already stated that the speed of the angels is 670 million miles per hour, the same as the speed of the light, which is the maximum speed possible.

Stand in Ranks:
According to the Holy Quran[d] the angels arrange themselves in ranks in the service of God and work in perfect discipline and accord all the time.[2] Probably this ranking is based on their power. The statement of Prophet Muhammad[SAW] explains that they arrange themselves in rows.[e]

Form Straight Line:
The statements[d,e] also suggest that the angels form a perfect straight line. The electromagnetic waves travel in straight line in

---

[d] By those who range themselves in ranks (or rows) (*saff*). (37:1)

(Those ranged in ranks say): "Not one of us but has a place appointed. And we are verily ranged in ranks (for service)." (37:164-165)

Then arrange to do (the commands of their Lord). (79:5)

[e] The Messenger of God (peace be upon him) said: Why don't you draw yourselves up in rows as angels do in the presence of their Lord? We said: Messenger of God, how do the angels draw themselves up in rows in the presence of their Lord? He (the Prophet) said: They make the first rows complete and keep close together in the row. (Muslim 864)

the form of wave.³ Since the angels are made from photons, they should also form perfect straight line.

Invisible:
We, the humans, do not have the ability to see the electromagnetic waves with our eyes. We are surrounded by electromagnetic waves, which can be converted into voice in radio and cellular or cordless phone and picture on television. Even the light we call visible light is invisible to our eyes. When light fall on an object, we do not see the light waves traveling from the source to the object. We only have the ability to see the object as a result of the interaction of the light, reflected from the object, with the retina.⁴ Had we had the ability to see the light wave, we would have been seeing the whole lighted area filled with light waves, but all we see is an empty space and the objects from which the light is reflected. The same is true for moon, which reflects sunlight. Even the light bulb, from which we see light emanating, we only see the glow of the element in the bulb, which is the result of light energy heating up the element. The same is true for sun and stars. Since the angels behave in a manner similar to the electromagnetic waves, we cannot see them in their original form. We can only see them when they transform themselves into human form.[f] We, the humans, will probably be able to see the angels at the time of death.[g]

---

[f] They say: "Why is not an angel sent down to him?" If We did send down an angel the matter would be settled at once and no respite would be granted them. If We had made it an angel We should have sent him as a man and We should certainly have caused them confusion in a matter which they have already covered with confusion. (6:8-9)

[g] If you could see, when the angels take souls of the unbelievers (at death). (How) they smite their faces and their backs, (saying): "Taste the Penalty of the blazing fire. (8:50)

But how (will it be) when the angels take their souls at death, and smite their faces and their backs. (47:27)

How the wicked (do fare) in the flood of confusion at death - the angels stretch forth their hands, (saying), "Yield up your souls. This day shall you receive your reward - a penalty of shame, for that you used to tell lies against God, and scornfully to reject of His Signs!" (6:93)

Those whose lives the angels take in a state of wrongdoing to their souls. Then would they offer submission (with the pretense), 'We did no evil (knowingly)." (The angels will reply), "Nay, but verily God knows all that you did; so enter the gates of Hell, to dwell therein. Thus evil indeed is the abode of the arrogant." (16:28-29)

When angels take the souls of those who die in sin against their souls they say: "In what (plight) were you?" They reply: "Weak and oppressed were we in the earth." They say: "Was not the earth of God spacious enough for you to move yourselves away (from evil)?" Such men will find their abode in Hell what an evil refuge! (4:97)

Who is more unjust than one who invents a lie against God or rejects his signs? For such their portion appointed must reach them from the Book (of decrees); until when Our messengers (of death) arrive and take their souls they say: "where are the things that you used to invoke besides God?" They will reply "they have left us in the lurch" and they will bear witness against themselves that they had rejected God. He will say: "enter you in the company of the peoples who passed away before you men and Jinns into the fire. (7:37-38)

Those whose lives the angels take in a state of purity, saying (to them), "Peace be on you, enter you the Garden, because of (the good) which you did (in the world). (16:32)

God's Messenger (peace be upon him) said, "The angels are present with one who dies, and if a man is good they say, 'Come out, good soul, which was in the good body; come out praiseworthy and be happy with rest and provision and a Lord Who is not angry.' That continues to be said to it till it comes out. It is then taken up to Heaven and the door is opened for it. The angels are asked who this is and reply that he is so and so, whereupon these words are spoken: 'Welcome, good soul, which was in the good body; enter praiseworthy and be happy with rest and provision and a Lord Who is not angry.' That continues to be said to it till it comes to the Heaven where God is. But when it is a bad man what is said is, 'Come out, wicked soul, which was in the wicked body; come out blameworthy and be grieved by a boiling liquid, one dark and intensely cold, and other kinds of its type.' That continues to be said to it till it comes out. It is then taken up to Heaven and the door is asked to

Reports suggest that Prophet Muhammad^{SAW}, however, had the ability to see the angels in their original form.^{h} As mentioned in Chapter 17 (The Origin of the Angels), at least on two occasions Prophet Muhammad^{SAW} saw Angel Gabriel (Jibraeel^{AS}) in his original form.^{i} The first vision took place at Jabl-Noor and the second vision took place when Prophet Muhammad^{SAW} went on Mi'raj (Ascension)^7

Imperceptibility:
We are surrounded by electromagnetic forces, but we do not seem to feel them by our senses. We can, therefore, state that the angels, whose physical behavior should be the same as electromagnetic forces, are imperceptible.

Penetrative Ability:
The penetrative power of the electromagnetic force depends upon the energy and therefore frequency of the electromagnetic wave. Higher the frequency, higher will be the penetrative power of the electromagnetic force. The visible light can penetrate transparent objects. X-rays can penetrate flesh but not bones.

---

be opened for it. The question will be asked who this is and the reply given that it is so and so, whereupon these words are spoken: 'There is no welcome for the wicked soul which was in the wicked body; go back blameworthy, for the gates of Heaven will not be opened for you.' It will then be sent away from Heaven and come to the grave." (Al-Tirmidhi 1627)

^{h} I see that which you do not. The Heaven cries (on account of the heavy load of the angels prostrating) and is justified in doing so. There is not a space equal to four fingers in it but is occupied by angels who are prostrating before God. (Al-Tirmidhi 406)

^{i} Prophet Muhammad once saw the Angel Gabriel (Jibraeel^{AS}) with six hundred wings. (Bukhari, Muslim, Tirmidhi)^5

Prophet Muhammad had seen Angel Gabriel (Jibraeel^{AS}) twice in his real shape: he had six hundred wings and had covered the whole horizon. (Tirmidhi)^6

Thus depending upon the energy of photons the angels are made from, they could have different penetrative ability.

Transformation into Human Form:
The Holy Quran and the statement of Prophet Muhammad^{SAW} cite instances when angels appeared in human form.[j] According

---

[j] Relate in the Book (the story of) Mary when she withdrew from her family to a place in the East. She placed a screen (to screen herself) from them: then We sent to her Our angel and he appeared before her as a man in all respects. (19:16-17)

Has the story reached you of the honored guests of Abraham? Behold they entered His presence and said: "Peace!" He said "Peace!" (and thought "these seem) unusual people." Then he turned quickly to his household brought out a fatted calf. And placed it before them... He said "Will you not eat?" (When they did not eat) He conceived a fear of them. They said "Fear not" and they gave him glad tidings of a son endowed with knowledge. But his wife came forward (laughing) aloud: she smote her forehead and said: "a barren old woman!" They said "Even so has your Lord spoken: and He is full of Wisdom and Knowledge." (Abraham) said: "And what O you Messengers is your errand (now)?" They said "We have been sent to a people (deep) in sin. "To bring on them (a shower of) stones of clay (brimstone). Marked as from your Lord for those who trespass beyond bounds." Then We evacuated those of the Believers who were there. But We found not there any just (Muslim) persons except in one house. And We left there a Signs for such as fear the Grievous Penalty. (51:24-37, also 15:51-60)

One day while God's Apostle was sitting with the people, a man came to him walking and said, "O God's Apostle. What is Belief?" The Prophet said, "Belief is to believe in God, His Angels, His Books, His Apostles, and the meeting with Him, and to believe in the Resurrection." The man asked, "O God's Apostle. What is Islam?" The Prophet replied, "Islam is to worship God and not worship anything besides Him, to offer prayers perfectly, to pay the (compulsory) charity, i.e. Zakat, and to fast the month of Ramadan." The man again asked, "O God's Apostle. What is Ihsan (i.e. perfection or benevolence)?" The Prophet said, "Ihsan is to worship God as if you see Him, and if you do not achieve this state of devotion, then (take it for granted that) God sees you." The man further asked, "O God's Apostle. When will the Hour be established?"

to Einstein's famous energy equation ($E=mc^2$), energy can be converted into mass and mass can be converted into energy. The angels being made from energy and being the forces of nature (see Appendix C), may have the ability to transform themselves from energy being to a mass being and back into energy being.

Space Adventure:
Unlike humans, the angels are not just consigned to the earth. They are spread out through out the universe.[k] They are in constant mode of both ascension towards heaven and descent from heaven.[l]

The Prophet replied, "The one who is asked about it does not know more than the questioner does, but I will describe to you its portents. When the lady slave gives birth to her mistress, that will be of its portents; when the bare-footed naked people become the chiefs of the people, that will be of its portents. The Hour is one of five things which nobody knows except God. Verily, the knowledge of the Hour is with God (alone). He sends down the rain, and knows that which is in the wombs." (31.34) Then the man left. The Prophet said, "Call him back to me." They went to call him back but could not see him. The Prophet said, "That was Gabriel who came to teach the people their religion." (See Hadith No. 47 Vol 1) (Bukhari 6.300)

[k] I see that which you do not. The Heaven cries (on account of the heavy load of the angels prostrating) and is justified in doing so. There is not a space equal to four fingers in it but is occupied by angels who are prostrating before God. (Al-Tirmidhi 406)

[l] The angels and the Spirit ascend unto Him in a Day the measure whereof is (as) fifty thousand years (70:4)

He does send down His angels with inspiration of His Command to such of His servants as He pleases (saying): "Warn (Man) that there is no god but I: so do your duty unto Me." (16:2)

(The angels say:) "We descend not but by command of your Lord: to Him belongs what is before us and what is behind us and what is between: and your Lord never does forget"

"Lord of the heavens and of the earth and of all that is between them: so worship Him and be constant and patient in His worship: knows you of any who is worthy of the same Name as He?" (19:64-65)

Summary:
The physical characteristics of the angels should be dictated by the physical characteristics of the electromagnetic forces. Many of these characteristics are confirmed by the statements made in the Holy Quran and by Prophet Muhammad^{SAW}. Their shape should be that of a wave and the size should be dictated by the frequency of the wave they correspond to. They form straight line. They glide throughout the universe at the speed of light. Their energy, power, and penetrative ability will depend upon the frequency of the photons they are made from. Higher the frequency, higher will be the energy, power, and penetrative

---

The Day the heaven shall be rent asunder with clouds and angels shall be sent down descending (in ranks) (25:25)

In the case of those who say "Our Lord is God" and further stand straight and steadfast the angels descend on them (from time to time): "Fear you not!" (they suggest) "nor grieve! but receive the Glad Tidings of the Garden (of Bliss) the which you were promised!

"We are your protectors in this life and in the Hereafter: therein shall you have all that your souls shall desire; therein shall you have all that you ask for!

"A hospitable gift from One Oft-Forgiving Most Merciful!" (41:30-32)

We have indeed revealed this (Message) in the night of Power. And what will explain to you what the Night of Power is? The Night of Power is better than a thousand Months. Therein come down the angels and the Spirit by God's permission on every errand: Peace!... This until the rise of Morn! (97:1-5)

The Prophet said, "Angels keep on descending from and ascending to the Heaven in turn, some at night and some by daytime, and all of them assemble together at the time of the Fajr and 'Asr prayers. Then those who have stayed with you overnight ascend unto God Who asks them, and He knows the answer better than they, "How have you left My slaves?" They reply, "We have left them praying as we found them praying." If anyone of you says "Amin" (during the prayer at the end of the recitation of Surat-al-Fatiha), and the angels in Heaven say the same, and the two sayings coincide, all his past sins will be forgiven." (Bukhari 4.446 also 9.578, 1.530)

ability. They are invisible and imperceptible to humans. They have the ability to transform themselves into human form.

Chapter 19
The Biological Characteristics of the Angels

The angels are living beings. Living organism, according to scientific definition, has limited life span, consume food, procreate, and do purposeful work. In this chapter we will explore the biological characteristics of the angels.

Time of Appearance:
Since we made a case that the angels are made from photons whose physical characteristics are dictated by electromagnetic waves, we will explore when electromagnetic wave or force came into existence. According to the most recent cosmological model (Inflationary Cosmological Model and Big Bang Model) [1], the creation of universe started about 15 billion years ago. The model suggests that the electromagnetic force became an independent force only around 10^{-10} seconds after the bang, when the temperature dropped down to 10^{15} Kelvin. Even then the movement of photons was restricted due to frequent collision with charged particles. Only after three hundred thousand years [2], with the formation of atoms, the photons could travel 'unhindered and the full expanse of the universe.' Since free movement is one of the characteristics of the angels, we propose that the angels could have appeared about a million years after the big bang. Whereas the human being came into existence only about a million or two years ago, the Jinns probably about 4.8 billion years ago (soon after the creation of the earth), the angels could have come into existence about 15 billion years ago (within one million years after the bang).

Life Span:
The Holy Quran states that the angels and Gabriel (Jibraeel[AS]) (*Ar-Rooh*) descend on the 'Night of Power (*Lailatul-Qadr*)'.[a] The

---

[a] We have indeed revealed this (Message) in the night of Power. And what will explain to you what the Night of Power is? The Night of

Secrets of Angels, Demons, Satan, and Jinns

Night of Power falls in the month of Ramadhan. As long as this universe, at least the solar system, is in existence, the month of Ramadhan will be repeating itself every year and so would the Night of Power. Since Gabriel (Jibraeel^{AS}) and the angels descend on this night, they will keep on descending until the end of the Universe. The verse thus implies that Gabriel (Jibraeel^{AS}) and the angels will live until the end of the universe.

Israfeel^{AS}, the angel who is responsible for blowing the Trumpet that will mark the end of this world, has been waiting to fulfill his responsibility ever since he has been created.[b] The statement of Prophet Muhammad^{SAW} implies that Israfeel^{AS} will live until the end of this world.

Izraeel^{AS} who, along with his associates (see chapters 22 and 23), is responsible for taking our souls at the time of death will keep on doing his job until any soul is alive.[c]

When Adam^{AS} and Eve (Hawwa^{AS}) were in the Garden, one of the arguments Satan used to persuade them to eat from the forbidden tree was that they would become angel and live forever.[d] The Quranic statements suggest that the angels will live

---

Power is better than a thousand Months. Therein come down the angels and the Spirit (*Ar-Rooh*) by God's permission on every errand. Peace!... This until the rise of Morn! (97:1-5)

[b] God's Messenger (peace be upon him) said, "God created Israfil who has been keeping his feet in line from the day he was created and not raising his glance. Between him and the Lord Who is Blessed and Exalted, there are seventy lights, not one of which he could approach without being burned.". (Tirmidhi 5731)

[c] Say: "The Angel of Death, put in charge of you, will (duly) take your souls. Then shall you be brought back to your Lord," (32:11)

[d] We said: "O Adam! Dwell you and your wife in the garden and eat of the bountiful things therein as (where and when) you will but approach not this tree or you run into harm and transgression." (2-35, 7-19)

Then We said: "O Adam! Verily this is an enemy to you and your wife: so let him not get you both out of the Garden so that you are landed in misery. There is therein (enough provision) for you not to go hungry

Secrets of Angels, Demons, Satan, and Jinns

forever (i.e. until the end of universe). Probably Adam^{AS} knew this fact and Satan capitalized on human weakness to persuade him to eat from the forbidden tree.

According to the Holy Quran, the Day of Judgment will begin with the blowing of a Trumpet.^{e} According to the

---

nor to go naked. Nor to suffer from thirst nor from the sun's heat " (20-117, 118, 119)

Then began Satan to whisper suggestions to them bringing openly before their minds all their shame that was hidden from them (before). (7-20)

He said " O Adam! Shall I lead you to Tree of Eternity and to a kingdom that never decays?" (20-120) "Your Lord only forbade you this tree lest you should become angels or such beings as live for ever." (7-20) And he swore to them both that he was their sincere adviser. (7-21)

^{e} And the Day that the Trumpet will be sounded then will be smitten with terror those who are in the heavens and those who are on the earth except such as God will please (to exempt): and all shall come to His (Presence) as beings conscious of their lowliness. (27:87)

The Trumpet will (just) be sounded when all that are in the heavens and on the earth will swoon except such as it will please God (to exempt). Then will a second one be sounded when behold they will be standing and looking on! (39:68)

One day the Earth will be changed to a different Earth and so will be the Heavens and (men) will be marshaled forth before God the One the Irresistible; (14:48)

The Day when the Trumpet will be sounded: that Day We shall gather the sinful blear-eyed (with terror) (20:102)
Then when the Trumpet is blown there will be no more relationships between them that day nor will one ask after another! (23:101)

It is He who created the heavens and the earth in true (proportions): the day He says "Be" Behold! it is. His Word is the truth. His will be the dominion the day the trumpet will be blown. He knows the Unseen as well as that which is open. For He is the Wise well acquainted (with all things). (6:73)

scholars[3,4], when the first Trumpet will be blown everyone and everything will be destroyed. When the second Trumpet will be blown, everyone shall be brought back to life. According to the statement[5] of Prophet Muhammad[SAW], Gabriel (Jibraeel[AS]), Michael (Mikaeel[AS]), Israfeel[AS] and Izraeel[AS] and those angels carrying the Throne of God will not die after the first blow, but will die later.[f]

According to Einstein's theory of relativity a moving clock ticks slower than a stationary clock.[6] Logic suggests that, if the time elapses more slowly for an individual in motion than it does for a stationary individual, the individual in motion should be able to live longer than the stationary individual. After all, the time measured by heartbeat and the decay of body parts will also slow down for the individual in motion. Although this phenomenon has not been confirmed for humans, it has been confirmed for muons. The stationary muons disintegrate in two millionth of a second. But if these muons are traveling at a speed of 667 million miles per hour (99.5% of the light speed), their lifetime is seen to increase ten folds. Since the time for muons traveling at a speed of 667 million miles per hour will slow down by a factor of ten, their lifetime increases by the same factor. The logic suggests that the time for photon, moving at the speed of light, will stand still. According to Greene, 'light, which is made up of photon, does not get old: a photon that emerged form big bang (about 15 billion years ago) is the same age today as it was then.'[7] The same can be said about the angels who are made from photons and are moving at the speed of light. They do not get old and should not die until the end of universe.

As mentioned earlier, the creation of universe started from a 'primordial point' about 15 billion years ago with a big bang[g], 'which spewed forth all of space and all matter'.[8,9] Ever

---

--- the trumpet will be blown and We shall collect them all together. (18:99)

[f] All that is on the earth will perish. But will abide (forever) the Face of your Lord – Full of Majesty, Bounty and Honor. (55:26-27)
[g] With the power and skill did We construct the Firmament: for it is We Who create the vastness of Space. (51:47)

since the big bang the universe is expanding.[10] The scientists do not know if the universe will continue to expand indefinitely or the expansion will come to halt and then will start contracting. If the average matter density of the universe exceeds certain value (10^{-29} grams per cubic centimeter), then the universe will start contracting. If contraction starts, the universe will begin to collapse upon itself. All the galaxies will start to approach one another, first slowly and then at a blinding speed. Eventually it will collapse into a primordial point.[11] The Holy Quran favors the collapsing scenario.[h] In that case the electromagnetic force along with the other three fundamental forces (the strong, weak, and gravitational force) [12] will collapse into one super or grand force. Since these forces will cease to exist as individual forces, the angels will also cease to exist. Thus the collapse of the fundamental forces will mark the death of all the angels.

The universe was created about 15 billion years ago. Since the angels will not die until the end of the universe, and they were created within one million years of the creation of the universe, each of them is about 15 billion years old. Their life span is the age of the Universe.

Food:

The Holy Quran suggests that the angels do not consume human food.[i] Angels, who appeared suddenly before Ibraheem[AS] in the guise of men,[13] refused to eat the meal he prepared for them. It was a common belief of the unbelievers during the time of the

---

[h] The Day that we roll up the heavens like a scroll rolled up for books (completed) even as We produced the first Creation so shall We produce a new one: a promise We have undertaken: truly shall We fulfill it. (21:104)

[i] Has the story reached you of the honored guests of Abraham? Behold they entered His presence and said: "Peace!" He said "Peace!" (and thought "these seem) unusual people." Then he turned quickly to his household brought out a fatted calf. And placed it before them... He said "Will you not eat?" (When they did not eat) He conceived a fear of them. They said "Fear not" and they gave him glad tidings of a son endowed with knowledge. (51:24-28)

Prophets that only angels could be messengers because they do not eat.^j

---

^j And they say: "What sort of an apostle is this who eats food and walks through the streets? Why has not an angel been sent down to him to give admonition with him? (25:7)

And the apostles whom We sent before you were all (men) who ate food and walked through the streets: We have made some of you as a trial for others: will you have patience? For God is One Who sees (all things). (25:20)

Behold the apostles came to them from before them and behind them (preaching): "Serve none but God." They said "If our Lord had so pleased He would certainly have sent down angels (to preach): now we reject your mission (altogether)." (41:14)

(Further We sent a long line of prophets for your instruction.) We sent Noah to his people: he said "O my people! worship God! You have no other god but Him: will you not fear (Him)?" The chiefs of the Unbelievers among his people said: "He is no more than a man like yourselves: his wish is to assert his superiority over you: if God had wished (to send messengers) He could have sent down angels: never did we hear such a thing (as he says) among our ancestors of old." (23:23-24)

Such as fear not the meeting with Us (for Judgment) say: "Why are not the angels sent down to us or (why) do we not see our Lord?" Indeed they have an arrogant conceit of themselves and mighty is the insolence of their impiety! The Day they see the angels no joy will there be to the sinners that Day: the (angels) will say: "There is a barrier forbidden (to you) altogether!" (25:21-22)

What kept men back from Belief when Guidance came to them was nothing but this: they said "Has God sent a man like us) to be (His) Apostle?" Say "If there were settled on the earth angels walking about in peace and quiet We should certainly have sent them down from the heavens an angel for an apostle." (17:94-95)

Before you also the apostles we sent were but men to whom We granted inspiration: if you realize this not ask of those who possess the Message. Nor did We give them bodies that ate no food nor were they exempt from death. (21:7-8)

The life from the scientific perspective is of cellular origin. The basic unit of this life is cell. Some living organisms only consist of one cell. Most of the living organisms, however, are multicellular. The body of humans is composed of billions of cells. The primary food source for all the animals is plant, which is also of cellular nature. Whereas, herbivorous animals only consume plant, carnivorous animals consume other animals. Humans consume both plants and animals. Since humans and animals, which are of cellular origin, consume food composed of cells, logic suggests that the angels who are made from photons will consume photons as food.

Food serves two purposes. It maintains the animal body by replacing worn out cells, and provides energy for the animals to do purposeful work. Since angels do not get old (or deteriorate), they will not need food for maintenance purpose. They will, however, need food (photons) as a source of energy to do purposeful work.

Procreation:
With the passage of time the living organisms get old and die. The only way for a species to survive is procreation. Since the angels do not get old and will live until the end of the universe, they do not need to procreate.

Gender:
The living organisms procreate by sexual and asexual reproduction. The organisms that reproduce asexually are unisexual. Their children are identical to the mother. The organisms that reproduce sexually have genders. The gender adds to the diversity. The children inherit genes from both the father and the mother. As such they inherit some features from the father side and some from the mother side. Since angels do not procreate, they should be asexual. They are probably neither male nor female. This could be one reason why the Holy Quran has condemned assigning female names to angels.[k] Another

---

[k] Those who believe not in the Hereafter name the angels with female names. But they have no knowledge therein. They follow nothing but conjecture; and conjecture avails nothing against Truth. (53:27-28)

reason for ridiculing this statement was their claim that God has daughters, implying that the angels are the daughters of God.[1]

Purposeful Work:
The work by definition requires energy. As will be shown later, the angels are busy day and night doing purposeful work. Humans and other animals, made from cells, draw energy by consuming food of cellular origin. Logic suggests that the angels, who are made from photons, will draw energy by consuming photons.

It is a common observation that most of the activity around the earth is based on the solar energy. It is the solar energy that puts the wind in motion and evaporates water from the ocean. The wind then carries water vapor in the sky to form cloud. As the rainwater flows through river, it moves boats, breaks rocks into sand, irrigates fields, produces electricity, and etc. The wind also drives the ships in ocean. It is the water and solar energy (and carbon dioxide) which produces vegetation, which is the source of food for animals. It is the wood (a form of dried vegetation) that used to be the source of energy in the past and still is in remote areas. It is also the vegetation buried under the earth for millions of years that is now used as coal, gas and oil. Most of the modern day communication is conducted through electromagnetic force. Electricity, which drives most of the communication equipment (radio, television, telephone, cellular phone and others) and the appliances is produced by hydropower, coal, or oil. Thus the source of most of the activity

---

And they make into females angels who themselves serve God. Did they witness their creation? Their evidence will be recorded and they will be called to account! (43:19)

Now ask them their opinion: is it that your Lord has (only) daughters and they have sons? Or that We created the angels female and they are witnesses (thereto)? Is it not that they say from their own invention. (37:149-151)

[1] Has then your Lord (O Pagans!) preferred for you sons and taken for Himself daughters among the angels? Truly you utter a most dreadful saying! (17:40)

on the earth is solar energy, which is basically a collection of photons. It is probably the angels who carry out all of this work by consuming photon. See Appendix C for a more detailed explanation.

Population:
The Quranic verse suggests that two guardian angels accompany each one of us.^{m} According to Prophet Muhammad^{SAW}, another angel accompanies us who advises us to do good.^{n} This adds up to three angels per person. Since the current human population is over six billion, there could be at least eighteen billion angels just accompanying humans.

Another statement of the Prophet Muhammad^{SAW} suggests that the angels occupy every bit of this universe.^{o} According to physicists, in every cubic meters of the universe there are, on average, about 400 million photons. A percentage of the "snow " we see on the television screen when the station sign off is due to this electromagnetic radiation.

According to another statement of Prophet Muhammad^{SAW}, just like humans have worship centers on the earth, the angels have a worship center in the heaven, called *Bait-ul-Mamoor*. Every day 70,000 angels enter this house. There are so many angels in the Universe that every angel will only get one opportunity to worship in this house in his life

---

^{m} Behold two (guardian angels) appointed to learn (his doings) learn (and note them) one sitting on the right and one on the left. Not a word does he utter but there is a sentinel by him ready (to note it). (50:17-18)

^{n} Every human being has two houses in his heart. In one house lives an angel and in the other house lives satan (evil Jinn). The angel persuades him to do good deeds and the Satan persuades him to do bad deeds. When he is busy remembering God, the satan backs off. When he is not busy in remembrance of God, the Satan persuades him to do bad deeds.^{14}

^{o} I see that which you do not. The Heaven cries (on account of the heavy load of the angels prostrating) and is justified in doing so. There is not a space equal to four fingers in it but is occupied by angels who are prostrating before God. (Al-Tirmidhi 406)

lifetime.[15] Since the angels have been in existence for almost 15 billion years, about 380 trillion angels have already prayed in this house. Even if we assume that the Universe will at least last for one more billion years, the population of the angels could be at least 400 trillion.

Summary:
The angels are living beings. Living organism, according to scientific definition, has limited life span, consume food, procreate, and do purposeful work. The Quranic statements and our scientific understanding of their nature suggest that all the angels were probably born about a million years after the creation of the universe and will not die until the end of the universe. They do not procreate and have no gender. Considering that they are energy beings, they consume photons to do purposeful work. The population of angels is estimated to be at least 400 trillion.

Chapter 20
The Intellectual Ability of the Angels

The human being is the most intelligent species we know of. It is the faculties of speaking, hearing, sight, intelligence, and affection that distinguish humans from the rest of the animals.[a] Human uniqueness usually centers on the gift of speech: 'our faculty of using signs and symbols to stand for things and then to construct abstract or imaginary worlds beyond the here and now.'[1] It is the most powerful channel of communication in the world of nature. It can carry vastly more information, and at a much higher rate, than any other natural form of communication. Speech enables humans to communicate with his fellow being and reasoning produces experiences. We will now explore what kind of intelligence the angels possess.

---

[a] He has created man. He has taught him speech (and intelligence). (55:3-4)

It is He who brought you forth from the wombs of your mothers when you knew nothing; and He gave you hearing (*samaa*) and sight (*absaara*) and intelligence and affection (*afeedatah*) that you may give thanks (to God). (16:78)

It is He who created (*anshaa*) for you (the faculties of) hearing (*samaa*), seeing (*absaara*), feeling, and understanding (*afeedatah*). Little thanks it is you give. (23:78)

It is He who has created you (and made you grow) (*anshaa*), and made (*jaala*) for you the faculties of hearing (*samaa*), seeing (*absaara*), feeling, and understanding (*afeedatah*). Little thanks it is you give. (67:23)

Read (*iqra*)! in the name of Your Lord and Cherisher, who created. Created man out of a (mere) clot of congealed blood. Proclaim! and Your Lord is most bountiful. He who taught (the use of) the Pen - Taught man (*al-insaan*) which he knew not. (96:1-5)

The Power of Communication:
According to Quranic verses, the angels, like humans, also seem to possess the power of communication. We know[b] that Gabriel (Jibraeel[AS]) brought the Holy Quran to Prophet Muhammad[SAW]. This would not have been possible if he could not converse with Prophet Muhammad[SAW]. They can also communicate with humans in general after assuming human form.[c] They, according

---

[b] Verily this is the word of a most honorable Messenger. Endued with Power with rank before the Lord of the Throne. With authority there (and) faithful of his trust. (81:19-21)

By the Star when it goes down. Your Companion is neither astray nor being misled. Nor does he say (aught) of (his own) Desire. It is no less than inspiration sent down to him: He was taught by one mighty in Power. Endued with Wisdom: (53:1-6)

That this is verily the word of an honored apostle; (69:40)

[c] Relate in the Book (the story of) Mary when she withdrew from her family to a place in the East. She placed a screen (to screen herself) from them: then We sent to her Our angel and he appeared before her as a man in all respects. She said: "I seek refuge from you to (God) Most Gracious: (come not near) if you do fear God." He said: "Nay I am only a messenger from your Lord (to announce) to you the gift of a holy son." She said: "How shall I have a son seeing that no man has touched me and I am not unchaste?" He said: "So (it will be): your Lord says `That is easy for Me: and (We wish) to appoint him as a Sign unto men and a Mercy from Us': it is a matter (so) decreed." So she conceived him and she retired with him to a remote place. (19:16-22)

Has the story reached you of the honored guests of Abraham? Behold they entered His presence and said: "Peace!" He said "Peace!" (and thought "these seem) unusual people." Then he turned quickly to his household brought out a fatted calf. And placed it before them... He said "Will you not eat?" (When they did not eat) He conceived a fear of them. They said "Fear not" and they gave him glad tidings of a son endowed with knowledge. But his wife came forward (laughing) aloud: she smote her forehead and said: "a barren old woman!" They said "Even so has your Lord spoken: and He is full of Wisdom and Knowledge." (Abraham) said: "And what O you Messengers is your errand (now)?" They said "We have been sent to a people (deep) in sin.

to Prophet Muhammad^{SAW}, can also communicate with humans through thoughts and give them ideas and suggestions.^{d} As mentioned in Chapter 18, the angels, being an energy being, could have strong penetrating power. They may be able to penetrate the human body and blood stream. Once in the blood stream they can reach any part of human body. They also have the ability to communicate with God. The Holy Quran describes many instances where they communicated or will communicate with God.^{e}

"To bring on them (a shower of) stones of clay (brimstone). Marked as from your Lord for those who trespass beyond bounds." Then We evacuated those of the Believers who were there. But We found not there any just (Muslim) persons except in one house. And We left there a Signs for such as fear the Grievous Penalty. (51:24-37 also 15:51-60)

^{d} Every human being has two houses in his heart. In one house lives an angel and in the other house lives Satan (evil Jinn). The angel persuades him to do good deeds and the Satan persuades him to do bad deeds. When he is busy remembering God, the Satan backs off. When he is not busy in remembrance of God, the Satan persuades him to do bad deeds.^{2}

^{e} Behold your Lord said to the angels: "I will create a vicegerent on the earth." They said "Wilt you place therein one who will make mischief therein and shed blood? Whilst we do celebrate your praises and glorify your holy (name)?" He said: "I know what you know not."

And He taught Adam the nature of all things; then He placed them before the angels and said: "Tell Me the nature of these if you are right."

They said: "Glory to you of knowledge we have none save that you have taught us: in truth it is you who art perfect in knowledge and wisdom."

He said: "O Adam! Tell them their natures." When he had told them God said: "Did I not tell you that I know the secrets of heaven and the earth and I know what you reveal and what you conceal?"

And behold We said to the angels: "Bow down to Adam"; and they bowed down not so Iblees he refused and was haughty he was of those who reject Faith. (2:30-34)

God's Messenger (peace be upon him) said: Our Lord is pleased with

Ability to See Humans:

The angels can see us, but we cannot see them. Had they not be able to see us, they would not be able to guard us and record our deeds.[f]

---

two men: One man who gets up from his bed and his quilt (parting) from his comfort and his wife for prayer. God says to His angels: Look at My servant, he got out of bed, his quilt (parting himself) from his comfort and his wife for the sake of prayer with an earnest desire for that which is with Me and out of fear of what is with Me. And a person who fights for the sake of God and retreats along with his companions, knowing what burden is there upon him for this retreat (and what reward is there for him) in returning (to fight). So he returns till his blood is shed and God says to the angels: Look at My servant, he returned with (the earnest) desire for that which is with Me, and out of fear of what is with Me till his blood was spilt. (Tirmidhi 1251)

God's Messenger (peace be upon him) said, 'When the day of Arafah comes God descends to the lowest heaven and praises them to the angels saying, "Look at my servants who have come to Me dishevelled, dusty and crying out from every deep valley. I call you to witness that I have forgiven them." The angels say, "My Lord, so and so was suspected of sin, also so and so and such and such a woman." He said that God Who is Great and Glorious, replied, "I have forgiven them." God's Messenger (peace be upon him) said, "on day have more people been set free from Hell than on the day of Arafah." (Tirmidhi 2601)

God's Apostle said, "Angels come to you in succession by night and day and all of them get together at the time of the Fajr and 'Asr prayers. Those who have passed the night with you (or stayed with you) ascend (to the Heaven) and God asks them, though He knows everything about you, well, "In what state did you leave my slaves?" The angels reply: "When we left them they were praying and when we reached them, they were praying." (Bukhari 1.530 also 4.446 and 9.578)

[f] But verily over you (are appointed angels) to protect you – Kind and Honorable writing down (your deeds). They know (and understand) all that you do. (82:10-12)

For each (such person) there are (angels) in succession before and behind him: they guard him by command of God. Verily never will God change the condition of a people until they change it themselves (with their own souls). But when (once) God wills a people's

Intelligence:
The angels, like humans, also possess intelligence. They use reasoning and observation to draw conclusions. It was only the power of reasoning that allowed them to conclude that human being will shed blood on the earth[g] when they raised objection against Adam[AS]

Knowledge:
The angels also seem to possess some type of knowledge.[h] But their knowledge is not at par with that of humans. According to

---

punishment there can be no turning it back nor will they find besides Him any to protect. (13:11)

He is the Irresistible (watching) from above over his worshippers and He sets guardians over you. At length when death approaches one of you Our angels take his soul and they never fail in their duty. (6:61)

Behold two (guardian angels) appointed to learn (his doings) learn (and note them) one sitting on the right and one on the left. Not a word does he utter but there is a sentinel by him ready (to note it). (50:17-18)

Or do they think that We hear not their secrets and their private counsels? Indeed (We do), and Our Messengers are by them, to record. (43:80)

But verily over you (are appointed angels) to protect you – Kind and Honorable writing down (your deeds). They know (and understand) all that you do. (82:10-12)

[g] Behold your Lord said to the angels: "I will create a vicegerent on the earth." They said "Wilt you place therein one who will make mischief therein and shed blood? Whilst we do celebrate your praises and glorify your holy (name)?" He said: "I know what you know not." (2:30)

[h] And He taught Adam the nature of all things; then He placed them before the angels and said: "Tell Me the nature of these if you are right."

They said: "Glory to you of knowledge we have none save that you have taught us: in truth it is you who art perfect in knowledge and wisdom."

Syed Maudoodi[2], it is possible that the knowledge of the individual angels is confined only to his own special department – air, water, cloud, etc. In contrast human knowledge is comprehensive.

Summary:
The angels, like human beings, have the power of observation and intelligence. They communicate with humans through their thought process and with prophets. They may also converse directly with human beings after acquiring human form. They can also communicate with God. They also possess knowledge, but it is not at par with that of humans.

He said: "O Adam! Tell them their natures." When he had told them God said: "Did I not tell you that I know the secrets of heaven and the earth and I know what you reveal and what you conceal?"

And behold We said to the angels: "Bow down to Adam"; and they bowed down not so Iblees he refused and was haughty he was of those who reject Faith. (2:30-34)

Chapter 21
The Spiritual Nature of the Angels

In this chapter we will explore the spiritual nature of the angels.

Free Will:
The angels do not have a will of their own. They only execute the commands of God.[a]

The Belief of the Angels:
The angels believe[b] in the Oneness of God and the Prophethood of Muhammad[SAW].

Serve only God:
The angels only serve God.[c]

---

[a] O you who believe! Save yourselves and your families from a Fire whose fuel is Men and Stones over which are (appointed) angels stern (and) severe who flinch not (from executing) the Commands they receive from God but do (precisely) what they are commanded. (66:6)

And to God does obeisance all that is in the heavens and on the earth whether moving (living) creatures or the angels: for none are arrogant (before their Lord). They all revere their Lord high above them and they do all that they are commanded. (16:49-50)

[b] There is no god but He: that is the witness of God His angels and those endued with knowledge standing firm on justice. There is no god but He the Exalted in Power the Wise. (3:18)
But God bears witness that what He has sent unto you He has sent from His (Own) Knowledge and the angels bear witness: but enough is God for a Witness. (4:166)

[c] And they make into females angels who themselves serve God. (43:19)

Hereafter:
Since the angels do not have a will of their own, there will be no reward or punishment for them in the Hereafter. As will be shown in the later chapter, they will be busy executing the commands of God in the Hereafter also.

Summary:
The angels do not have a will of their own. They only execute the commands of God and only serve Him. They believe in the Oneness of God and the Prophethood of Muhammad^{SAW}. They are busy day and night glorifying God. Since they do not have a free will, there will be no reward or punishment for them on the day of Judgement. They will be busy executing the commands of God in the Hereafter also.

Christ disdains not to serve and worship God nor do the angels those nearest (to God): those who disdain His worship and are arrogant He will gather them all together unto himself to (answer). (4:172)

To Him belong all (creatures) in the heavens and on the earth: even those who are in His (very) Presence (angels) are not too proud to serve Him nor are they (ever) weary (of His service). (21:19)

Chapter 22
The Functions of the Angels

The job of the angels is to execute the commands of God.[a] They are executing His commands in this world and will do the same in the Hereafter. Every angel has an assigned task.[b]

---

[a] And by those who glide along (on errands of mercy). Then press forward as in a race. Then arrange to do (the commands of their Lord) (79:3-5)

We send not the angels down except for just cause: if they came (to the ungodly) behold! no respite would they have! (15:8)

O you who believe! Save yourselves and your families from a Fire whose fuel is Men and Stones over which are (appointed) angels stern (and) severe who flinch not (from executing) the Commands they receive from God but do (precisely) what they are commanded. (66:6)

And to God does obeisance all that is in the heavens and on the earth whether moving (living) creatures or the angels: for none are arrogant (before their Lord). They all revere their Lord high above them and they do all that they are commanded. (16:49-50)

We have indeed revealed this (Message) in the night of Power: And what will explain to you what the Night of Power is? The Night of Power is better than a thousand Months. Therein come down the angels and the Spirit by God's permission on every errand: Peace!... This until the rise of Morn! (97:1-5)

To Him belong all (creatures) in the heavens and on the earth: even those who are in His (very) Presence are not too proud to serve Him nor are they (ever) weary (of His service. (21:19)

And they make into females angels who themselves serve God. (43:19)

The Prophet said, "O Gabriel, what prevents you from visiting us more often than you do?" Then this Verse was revealed: "And we angels descend not but by Command of your Lord. To Him belongs what is before us and what is behind us..." (19.64) So this was the answer to Muhammad. (Bukhari 4.441, 6.255, 9.547)

Their Role in This World:

The angels are probably the busiest creatures in the universe. They are busy executing a variety of tasks assigned to them by God.

Sustain the Throne of God
One of the functions of the angels is to sustain the throne of God.[c] We do not know the nature of this throne, but whatever it is, it is sustained by the angels.

Glorify God
They are busy day and night glorifying God.[d]

---

[b] (Those ranged in ranks say): "Not one of us but has a place appointed. And we are verily ranged in ranks (for service). And we are verily those who declare (God's) glory!" (37:164-166)

[c] Those who sustain the Throne (of God) and those around it sing Glory and Praise to their Lord; believe in Him; and implore forgiveness for those who believe. (40:7)

[d] They celebrate His praises night and day nor do they ever flag or intermit. (21:20)

Nay thunder repeats His praises and so do the angels with awe: (13:13)

Behold your Lord said to the angels: "I will create a vicegerent on the earth." They said "Will you place therein one who will make mischief therein and shed blood? While we do celebrate Your praises and glorify Your holy (name)?" He said: "I know what you know not." (2:30)

And to God does obeisance all that is in the heavens and on the earth whether moving (living) creatures or the angels: for none are arrogant (before their Lord). They all revere their Lord high above them and they do all that they are commanded. (16:49-50)

The heavens are almost rent asunder from above them (by His Glory): and the angels celebrate the Praises of their Lord and pray for

Messengers

One of the responsibilities of the angels in this world is to communicate the message of God to the humans.[e] There are few chosen angels responsible for this job.[f] They bring the message

---

forgiveness for (all) beings on the earth: Behold! Verily God is He the Oft-Forgiving Most Merciful. (42:5)

Christ disdains not to serve and worship God nor do the angels those nearest (to God): those who disdain His worship and are arrogant He will gather them all together unto himself to (answer). (4:172)

"And we are verily those who declare (God's) glory!" (37:166)

And you wilt see the angels surrounding the Throne (Divine) on all sides singing Glory and Praise to their Lord. The Decision between them (at Judgment) will be in (perfect) justice. And the cry (on all sides) will be "Praise be to God the Lord of the Worlds!" (39:75)

Those who sustain the Throne (of God) and those around it sing Glory and Praise to their Lord; believe in Him; and implore forgiveness for those who believe. (40:7)

But if they (Unbelievers) are arrogant (no matter): for in the presence of your Lord are those who celebrate His praises by night and by day. And they never flag (nor feel themselves above it). (41:38)

The Prophet (peace be upon him) said: I see that which you do not. The Heaven cries (on account of the heavy load of the angels prostrating) and is justified in doing so. There is not a space equal to four fingers in it but is occupied by angels who are prostrating before God. (Tirmidhi 406)

[e] He does send down His angels with inspiration of His Command to such of His servants as He pleases (saying): "Warn (Man) that there is no god but I: so do your duty unto Me." (16:2).

It is not fitting for a man that God should speak to him except by inspiration of from behind a veil or by the sending of a Messenger to reveal with God's permission what God wills: for He is Most High Most Wise. (42:51)

[f] Praise be to God Who created (out of nothing) the heavens and the earth Who made the angels messengers with wings two or three or four (Pairs): He adds to Creation as He pleases: for God has power over all things. (35:1)

to prophets as well as to few chosen such as Mary (Maryam^{AS}).^{g} Even the unbelievers were of the view that only angels bring the message or should at least accompany the messengers.^{h}

God chooses Messengers from angels and from men: for God is He Who hears and sees (all things). (22:75)

It is no less than inspiration sent down to him (Muhammad). He was taught by one mighty in Power (Gabriel/Jibraeel). Endued with Wisdom. (53:4-6)

^{g} Tell them about the guests of Abraham. When they entered his presence and said "Peace!" He said "We feel afraid of you!" They said: "Fear not! we give you glad tidings of a son endowed with wisdom." (15:51-53), see also (51:24-25, 28)

(The Messengers) said "O Loot! We are Messengers from your Lord! By no means shall they reach you! Now travel with your family while yet a part of the night remains and let not any of you look back: but your wife (will remain behind): to her will happen what happens to the people. Morning is their time appointed: is not the morning nigh?" (11:81)

At length when the messengers arrived among the adherents of Loot. He (Loot) said: "You appear to be uncommon folk."

They said: "Yea we have come to you to accomplish that of which they doubt. We have brought to you that which is inevitably due and assuredly we tell the truth. Then travel by night with your household when a portion of the night (yet remains) and do you bring up the rear. Let no one amongst you look back but pass on whither you are ordered." (15:61-66)

While he (Zakariyya) was standing in prayer in the chamber the angels called unto him: "God does give you glad tidings of Yahya witnessing the truth of a Word from God and (be besides) noble chaste and a Prophet of the (goodly) company of the righteous." (3:39)

Behold! The angels said: "O Maryam! God has chosen you and purified you; chosen you above the women of all nations. "O Mary! Worship your Lord devoutly; prostrate thyself and bow down (in prayer) with those who bow down." Behold! The angels said "O Maryam! God gives you glad tidings of a Word from Him: his name will be Christ Jesus the son of Mary held in honor in this world and the Hereafter and of (the company of) those nearest to God. He shall speak to the people in childhood and in maturity and he shall be (of the company) of the righteous." She said: "O my Lord! How shall I have a son when no man has touched me?" He said: "Even so: God creates what He wills; when He has decreed a plan He but said to it 'Be' and it is! And God will teach him the Book and Wisdom the Law and the Gospel. "And (appoint him) an Apostle to the Children of Israel (with this message): I have come to you with a sign from your Lord in that I make for you out of clay as it were the figure of a bird and breathe into it and it becomes a bird by God's leave; and I heal those born blind and the lepers and I quicken the dead by God's leave; and I declare to you what you eat and what you store in your houses. Surely therein is a Sign for you if you did believe. (I have come to you) to attest the Law, which was before me and to make lawful to you part of what was (before) forbidden to you; I have come to you with a Sign from your Lord. So fear God and obey me. It is God who is my Lord and your Lord; then worship Him. This is a way that is straight." (3:42-51)

Relate in the Book (the story of) Maryam when she withdrew from her family to a place in the East. She placed a screen (to screen herself) from them: then We sent to her Our angel and he appeared before her as a man in all respects. She said: "I seek refuge from you to (God) Most Gracious: (come not near) if you do fear God." He said: "Nay I am only a messenger from your Lord (to announce) to you the gift of a holy son." She said: "How shall I have a son seeing that no man has touched me and I am not unchaste?" He said: "So (it will be): Your Lord said 'That is easy for Me: and (We wish) to appoint him as a Sign unto men and a Mercy from Us': it is a matter (so) decreed." So she conceived him and she retired with him to a remote place. And the pains of childbirth drove her to the trunk of a palm-tree: she cried (in her anguish): "Ah! would that I had died before this! Would that I had been a thing forgotten and out of sight!" But (a voice) cried to her from beneath the (palm-free): "Grieve not! for your Lord has provided a rivulet beneath you. And shake towards thyself the trunk of the palm-tree: it will let fall fresh ripe dates upon you. So eat and drink and cool (your) eye. And if you do see any man say 'I have vowed a fast to (God) Most Gracious and this day will I enter into no talk with any human being.' " (19:16-26)

[h] "Then why are not gold bracelets bestowed on him (Moosa) or (why) come (not) with him angels accompanying him in procession?" (43:53)

They say: "We shall not believe in you until you cause spring to gush forth for us from the earth. Or (until) you have a garden of date trees

Guard Humans

Each human being is guarded and protected by two angels.[i] They are known as guardian angels.

---

and vines and cause rivers to gush forth in their midst carrying abundant water; Or you cause the sky to fall in pieces as you say (will happen) against us; or you bring God and the angels before (us) face to face; Or you have a house adorned with gold or you mount a ladder right into the skies. No we shall not even believe in you mounting until you send down to us a book that we could read."

Say: "Glory to my Lord! Am I aught but a man an apostle?"

What kept men back from Belief when Guidance came to them was nothing but this: they said "Has God sent a man like us) to be (His) Apostle?"

Say "If there were settled on the earth angels walking about in peace and quiet We should certainly have sent them down from the heavens an angel for an apostle." (16:90-95)

Such as fear not the meeting with Us (for Judgment) say: "Why are not the angels sent down to us or (why) do we not see our Lord?" Indeed they have an arrogant conceit of themselves and mighty is the insolence of their impiety! The Day they see the angels no joy will there be to the sinners that Day: the (angels) will say: "There is a barrier forbidden (to you) altogether!" (25:21-22)

---

[i] But verily over you (are appointed angels) to protect you – Kind and Honorable writing down (your deeds). They know (and understand) all that you do. (82:10-12)

For each (such person) there are (angels) in succession before and behind him: they guard him by command of God. Verily never will God change the condition of a people until they change it themselves (with their own souls). But when (once) God wills a people's punishment there can be no turning it back nor will they find besides Him any to protect. (13:11)

He is the Irresistible (watching) from above over his worshippers and He sets guardians over you. At length when death approaches one of you Our angels take his soul and they never fail in their duty. (6:61)

God's Apostle said, (A group of) angels stay with you at night and (another group of) angels by daytime, and both groups gather at the time of the 'Asr and Fajr prayers. Then those angels who have stayed

Recorders of Deeds

The guardian angels also record our deeds.[j] The one on the right records good deeds and the one on the left records bad deeds.

Test Human Character

Angels are also sent to test the character of a nation or individuals. For example, Haroot and Maroot were sent to test the Children of Israeel when they were living a life of captivity

---

with you overnight, ascend (to Heaven) and God asks them (about you)--and He knows everything about you. 'In what state did you leave My slaves?' The angels reply, 'When we left them, they were praying, and when we reached them they were praying.' " (Bukhari 9.525A, also Al-Muwatta 9.85)

[j] Behold two (guardian angels) appointed to learn (his doings) learn (and note them) one sitting on the right and one on the left. Not a word does he utter but there is a sentinel by him ready (to note it). (50:17-18)

Or do they think that We hear not their secrets and their private counsels? Indeed (We do), and Our Messengers are by them, to record. (43:80)

But verily over you (are appointed angels) to protect you – Kind and Honorable writing down (your deeds). They know (and understand) all that you do. (82:10-12)

in Babylon.[k] The angels were also sent to the people of Loot[AS] who were living in the sin of homosexuality as a final test.[l]

---

[k] They followed what the evil ones gave out (falsely) against the power of Solomon; the blasphemers were not Solomon but the evil ones teaching men magic and such things as came down at Babylon to the angels Haroot and Maroot. But neither of these taught anyone (such things) without saying: "We are only for trial so do not blaspheme." They learned from them the means to sow discord between man and wife. But they could not thus harm anyone except by God's permission. And they learned what harmed them not what profited them. And they knew that the buyers of (magic) would have no share in the happiness of the Hereafter. And vile was the price for which they did sell their souls if they but knew! (2:102)

[l] When Our Messengers came to Loot he was grieved on their account and felt himself powerless (to protect) them. He said: "This is a distressful day." And his people came rushing towards him and they had been long in the habit of practicing abominations. He said: "O my people! Here are my daughters: they are purer for you (if you marry)! Now fear God and cover me not with shame about my guests! Is there not among you a single right-minded man?" They said: "Well do you know we have no need of your daughters: indeed you know quite well what we want!" He said: "Would that I had power to suppress you or that I could betake myself to some powerful support." (The Messengers) said "O Loot! we are Messengers from your Lord! By no means shall they reach you! Now travel with your family while yet a part of the night remains and let not any of you look back: but your wife (will remain behind): to her will happen what happens to the people. Morning is their time appointed: is not the morning nigh?" When Our decree issued We turned (the cities) upside down and rained down on them brimstones hard as baked clay spread layer on layer marked as from your Lord: nor are they ever far from those who do wrong! (11:77-83)

At length when the messengers arrived among the adherents of Loot. He (Loot) said: "You appear to be uncommon folk." They said: "Yea we have come to you to accomplish that of which they doubt. We have brought to you that which is inevitably due and assuredly we tell the truth. Then travel by night with your household when a portion of the night (yet remains) and do you bring up the rear. Let no one amongst you look back but pass on whither you are ordered." And We made

Serve as Witness

The angels also bear witness[m] to the Oneness of God and the Prophethood of Muhammad[SAW]

Repel Evil

The angels are very prompt in repelling evil.[n] They check and frustrate evil wherever they find it and they are strengthened in this effort by their discipline and their ranging themselves in ranks.[1]

Help the Good People

The angels were sent to strengthen the prophets.[o] For example, God sent Angel Gabriel to support and strengthen Prophet Jesus

---

known this decree to him that the last remnants of those (sinners) should be cut off by the morning. The inhabitants of the City came in (mad) joy (at news of the young men). Loot said: "These are my guests: disgrace me not. But fear God and shame me not." They said: "Did we not forbid you (to speak) for all and sundry?" He said: "There are my daughters (to marry). If you must act (so)." Verily by your life (O Prophet) in their wild intoxication they wander in distraction to and fro. But the (mighty) Blast overtook them before morning. And We turned (the Cities) upside down and rained down on them brimstones hard as baked clay. Behold! in this are Signs for those who by tokens do understand. And the (cities were) right on the highroad. Behold! in this is a Sign for those who believe! (15:61-77)

[m] There is no god but He: that is the witness of God His angels and those endued with knowledge standing firm on justice. There is no god but He the Exalted in Power the Wise. (3:18)

But God bears witness that what He has sent unto you He has sent from His (Own) Knowledge and the angels bear witness: but enough is God for a Witness. (4:166)

[n] And so are strong in repelling (evil) (37:2)

[o] Those apostles We endowed with gifts some above others: to one of them God spoke; others He raised to degrees (of honor); to Jesus the

(Isa^{AS}) during his prophethood. The angels also help the believers.^p For examples, they helped the believers in battles during the time of Prophet Muhammad^{SAW}.

---

son of Mary We gave clear (Signs) and strengthened him with the Holy Spirit (*Rooh-al-Quds*). If God had so willed succeeding generations would not have fought among each other after clear (Signs) had come to them but they (chose) to wrangle some believing and others rejecting. If God had so willed they would not have fought each other; but God fulfills His plan. (2:253)

We gave Moses the Book and followed him up with a succession of Apostles; We gave Jesus the son of Mary clear (Signs) and strengthened him with the Holy Spirit (*Rooh-al-Quds*). Is it that whenever there comes to you an Apostle with what you yourselves desire not you are puffed up with pride? Some you called impostors and others you slay! (2:87)

Then will God say: "O Jesus the son of Mary! recount my favor to you and to your mother. Behold! I strengthened you with the Holy Spirit (*Rooh-al-Quds*) so that you did speak to the people in childhood and in maturity. Behold! I taught you the Book and Wisdom the Law and the Gospel. And behold! you make out of clay as it were the figure of a bird by My leave and you breath into it and it becomes a bird by My leave and you heal those born blind and the lepers by My leave. And behold! You bring forth the dead by My leave. And behold! I did restrain the Children of Israel from (violence to) you when you did show them the Clear Signs and the unbelievers among them said: `This is nothing but evident magic'. (5:110)

^p Remember you implored the assistance of your Lord and He answered you: "I will assist you with a thousand of the angels ranks on ranks." (8:9)

Remember your Lord inspired the angels (with the message): "I am with you: give firmness to the believers: I will instill terror into the hearts of the unbelievers: smite you above their necks and smite all their finger-tips off them." (8:12)

Remember that morning you did leave the household (early) to post the faithful at their stations for battle (of Uhd): and God hears and knows all things. Remember two of your parties meditated cowardice; but God was their Protector and in God should the faithful (ever) put their trust. God had helped you at Badr when you were a contemptible little force;

Comfort Good People
The angels give comfort to the good people in adversity.[q]

Implore Forgiveness for Good People
The angels implore forgiveness for the good people.[r]

---

then fear God; thus may you show your gratitude. Remember you said to the faithful: is it not enough for you that God should help you with three thousand angels (specially) sent down?
"Yea" if you remain firm and act aright even if the enemy should rush here on you in hot haste your Lord would help you with five thousand angels making a terrific onslaught. (3:121-125)

Their Prophet said to them: "God has appointed Taloot as king over you." They say: "How can he exercise authority over us when we are better fitted than he to exercise authority and he is not even gifted with wealth in abundance?" He said: "God has chosen him above you and has gifted him abundantly with knowledge and bodily prowess; God grants His authority to whom He pleases. God cares for all and He knows all things." And (further) their Prophet said to them: "A sign of his authority is that there shall come to you the Ark of the Covenant with (an assurance) therein of security from your Lord and the relics left by the family of Moses and the family of Aaron carried by angels. In this is a Symbol for you if you indeed have faith." (2:247-248)

But God did pour His calm on the apostle and on the believers and sent down forces which you saw not: He punished the unbelievers: thus does He reward those without faith. (9:26)

Gabriel came to the Prophet and said, "How do you look upon the warriors of Badr among yourselves?" The Prophet said, "As the best of the Muslims," or said a similar Statement. On that, Gabriel said, "And so are the Angels who participated in the Badr (battle)." (Bukhari 5.327)

[q] In the case of those who say "Our Lord is God" and further stand straight and steadfast the angels descend on them (from time to time): "Fear you not!" (they suggest) "nor grieve! but receive the Glad Tidings of the Garden (of Bliss) the which you were promised! We are your protectors in this life and in the Hereafter: therein shall you have all that your souls shall desire; therein shall you have all that you ask for! A hospitable gift from One Oft-Forgiving Most Merciful!" (41:30-32)

Send Peace and Blessing on Good People

It is also the job of the angels to send blessing[s] on the believers and Prophet Muhammad[SAW]. They also convey the blessing send by people to Prophet Muhammad[SAW].

---

[r] Those who sustain the Throne (of God) and those around it sing Glory and Praise to their Lord; believe in Him; and implore forgiveness for those who believe: "Our Lord! Your reach is over all things in Mercy and Knowledge. Forgive then those who turn in repentance and follow Your Path: and preserve them from the Penalty of the Blazing Fire!

"And grant our Lord! That they enter the Gardens of Eternity which You have promised to them and to the righteous among their fathers their wives and their posterity! For You art (He) the Exalted in Might Full of Wisdom.

"And preserve them from (all) ills; and any whom You does preserve from ills that Day on them will You have bestowed Mercy indeed: and that will be truly (for them) the highest Achievement. (40:7-9)

The heavens are almost rent asunder from above them (by His Glory): and the angels celebrate the Praises of their Lord and pray for forgiveness for (all) beings on the earth: Behold! Verily God is He the Oft-Forgiving Most Merciful. (42:5)

[s] O you who believe! Celebrate the praises of God and do this often and glorify Him morning and evening. He it is Who sends blessings on you as do His angels that He may bring you out from the depths of Darkness into Light: and He is Full of Mercy to the Believers. (33:41-43)

We have indeed revealed this (Message) in the night of Power. And what will explain to you what the Night of Power is? The Night of Power is better than a thousand Months. Therein come down the angels and the Spirit by God's permission on every errand. Peace!... This until the rise of Morn! (97:1-5)

God and His angels send blessings on the Prophet: O you that believe! Send you blessings on him and salute him with all respect. (33:56)

God's Apostle said, "The angels keep on asking for God's blessing and forgiveness for anyone of you as long as he is at his Musalla (praying place) and does not do Hadath (passes wind). The angels say, 'O God! Forgive him and be Merciful to him.' Each one of you is in the prayer

Curse the Evil Doers

The evil doers mess things up, which causes harm to the rest. Angels, therefore curse them.[t]

---

as long as he is waiting for the prayer and nothing but the prayer detains him from going to his family." (Bukhari 1.628, 1.436)

He who invokes blessings upon God's Messenger (peace be upon him) once, God and His Angels shower seventy blessings upon him. (Al-Tirmidhi 935)

God's Messenger (peace be upon him) said: There is a mobile (squads) of Angels on the earth convey to me the blessings invoked upon me by my Ummah. (Al-Tirmidhi 924)

God's Messenger (peace be upon him) said that when Laylat al-Qadr comes, Gabriel descends with a company of angels who invoke blessings on ever who is standing or sitting and remembering God, who is Great and Glorious. Then when their festival day comes, i.e. the day when they break their fast, God speaks proudly of them to His angels saying, "My angels, what is the reward of a hired servant who has fully accomplished his work?" They reply, "Our Lord, his reward is that he should be paid his wage in full." He says, "My angels, My male and female servants have fulfilled what I have made obligatory for them, and then have come out raising their voices in supplication. By My might, glory, honour, high dignity and exalted station, I shall certainly answer them." Then He says, "Return, for I have forgiven you and changed your evil deeds into good deeds." He said that they then returned having received forgiveness. (Tirmidhi 2096)

---

[t] Those who reject faith and die rejecting on them is God's curse and the curse of angels and of all mankind. They will abide therein: Their penalty will not be lightened nor will respite be their (lot). (2:161-162)

How shall God guide those who reject faith after they accepted it and bore witness that the Messenger was true and that clear signs had come to them? But God guides not a people unjust. Of such the reward is that on them (rests) the curse of God, of His angels, and of all mankind. (3:86-87)

Impose the Final Punishment on Evil Doers

The angels also impose the final punishment on people who refuse to listen to the prophets.[u]

---

[u] They say: "Why is not an angel sent down to him?" If We did send down an angel the matter would be settled at once and no respite would be granted them. (6:8)

Do the (ungodly) wait until the angels come to them or there comes the Command of your Lord (for their doom)? So did those who went before them. But God wronged them not: nay they wronged their own souls. (16:33)

They (the angels) said "We have been sent to a people (deep) in sin (the people of Loot). To bring on them (a shower of) stones of clay (brimstone). Marked as from your Lord for those who trespass beyond bounds." (51:32-34)

When Our decree issued We turned (the cities) upside down and rained down on them brimstones hard as baked clay spread layer on layer. Marked as from your Lord: nor are they ever far from those who do wrong! (11:82-83)

They (the angels) said: "We have been sent to a people (deep) in sin. Excepting the adherents of Loot: them we are certainly (charged) to save (from harm) all. Except his wife who we have ascertained will be among those who will lag behind." (15:58-60)

Never did We destroy a population that had not a term decreed and assigned beforehand. Neither can a people anticipate its Term nor delay it. They say: "O you to whom the Message is being revealed! Truly you are mad (or possessed)! Why bring you not angels to us if it be that you have the Truth?" We send not the angels down except for just cause: if they came (to the ungodly) behold! no respite would they have! (15:4-8)

See you one who forbids. A votary when he (turns) to pray? See you if He is on (the road of) Guidance? Or enjoins Righteousness? See you if he denies (Truth) and turns away? Know he not that God does see? Let him beware! If he desist not We will drag him by the forelock. A lying sinful forelock! Then let him call (for help) to his council (of comrades): We will call on the angels of punishment (to deal with him)! (96:9-18)

Take Soul Away at the Time of Death

Another responsibility of the angels is to draw out the soul of the humans at the time of death.[v] As mentioned earlier, the angels of

---

[v] He is the Irresistible (watching) from above over his worshippers and He sets guardians over you. At length when death approaches one of you Our angels take his soul and they never fail in their duty. (6:61)

Say: "The Angel of Death, put in charge of you, will (duly) take your souls. Then shall you be brought back to your Lord," (32:11)

By the (angels) who tear out (the souls of the wicked) with violence. By those who gently draw out (the souls of the blessed). (79:1-2)

If you could see, when the angels take souls of the unbelievers (at death). (How) they smite their faces and their backs, (saying): "Taste the Penalty of the blazing fire. (8:50)

But how (will it be) when the angels take their souls at death, and smite their faces and their backs. (47:27)

How the wicked (do fare) in the flood of confusion at death - the angels stretch forth their hands, (saying), "Yield up your souls. This day shall you receive your reward - a penalty of shame, for that you used to tell lies against God, and scornfully to reject of His Signs!" (6:93)

Those whose lives the angels take in a state of wrongdoing to their souls. Then would they offer submission (with the pretense), 'We did no evil (knowingly)." (The angels will reply), "Nay, but verily God knows all that you did; so enter the gates of Hell, to dwell therein. Thus evil indeed is the abode of the arrogant." (16:28-29)

When angels take the souls of those who die in sin against their souls they say: "In what (plight) were you?" They reply: "Weak and oppressed were we in the earth." They say: "Was not the earth of God spacious enough for you to move yourselves away (from evil)?" Such men will find their abode in Hell what an evil refuge! (4:97)

Who is more unjust than one who invents a lie against God or rejects his signs? For such their portion appointed must reach them from the Book (of decrees); until when Our messengers (of death) arrive and take their souls they say: "where are the things that you used to invoke besides God?" They will reply "they have left us in the lurch" and they

death treat the good and bad differently. They treat the good ones gently and the bad ones harshly.[w]

Question the Dead

When a person is buried, two angels enter his grave and question him about his past life.[x]

---

will bear witness against themselves that they had rejected God. He will say: "enter you in the company of the peoples who passed away before you men and Jinns into the fire. (7:37-38)

Those whose lives the angels take in a state of purity, saying (to them), "Peace be on you, enter you the Garden, because of (the good) which you did (in the world). (16:32)

[w] God's Messenger (peace be upon him) said, "The angels are present with one who dies, and if a man is good they say, 'Come out, good soul, which was in the good body; come out praiseworthy and be happy with rest and provision and a Lord Who is not angry.' That continues to be said to it till it comes out. It is then taken up to Heaven and the door is opened for it. The angels are asked who this is and reply that he is so and so, whereupon these words are spoken: 'Welcome, good soul, which was in the good body; enter praiseworthy and be happy with rest and provision and a Lord Who is not angry.' That continues to be said to it till it comes to the Heaven where God is. But when it is a bad man what is said is, 'Come out, wicked soul, which was in the wicked body; come out blameworthy and be grieved by a boiling liquid, one dark and intensely cold, and other kinds of its type.' That continues to be said to it till it comes out. It is then taken up to Heaven and the door is asked to be opened for it. The question will be asked who this is and the reply given that it is so and so, whereupon these words are spoken: 'There is no welcome for the wicked soul which was in the wicked body; go back blameworthy, for the gates of Heaven will not be opened for you.' It will then be sent away from Heaven and come to the grave." (Al-Tirmidhi 1627)

[x] Prophet Muhammad[SAW] said, 'When a human is laid in his grave and his companions return and he hears their footsteps, two angels will come to him and make him sit and ask him, "What did you say about this man, Muhammad, may peace be upon him?" He will say, "I testify that he is God's servant and His Messenger." Then it will be said to him, "Look at your place in Hell-Fire. God has exchanged for you a

place in Paradise instead of it".' The Prophet, peace be upon him, added, 'The dead person will see both his places. As for a non-believer or a hypocrite, he will respond to the angels, "I do not know, but I used to say what the people used to say ! " It will be said to him, "Neither did you know nor did you seek guidance from those who had knowledge." Then he will be hit with an iron hammer between his two ears, and he will cry and that cry will be heard by all except human beings and jinns'." (Bukhari and Muslim)

Prophet Muhammad[SAW] said, 'When a Muslim is questioned in his grave, he bears witness that there is no god but God, and that Muhammad is the Messenger of God.' According to one report, the verse, 'God will establish in strength those who believe with the Word, that stands firm in this world and in the Hereafter' (Qur'an 14.27) was revealed concerning the punishment of the grave. The deceased will be asked, 'Who is your Lord?' He will say, 'God is my Lord and Muhammad is my Prophet.' That is what is meant by the statement of God, 'God will make firm those who believe with a firm statement in this life and in the hereafter'." (Al-Bukhari, Muslim, and Sunan)[3]

Prophet Muhammad[SAW] said, "When a deceased person is laid in his grave, he hears the sound of the footsteps of people as they go away. If he is a believer, the prayer will stand by his head, the fasting will be to his right, alms to his left, and all other good deeds of charity, kindness to relations, and good behavior will be by his feet. The deceased will be questioned by the angels at his head. The prayer will say, 'There is no entrance through me.' Then he will be questioned by his right side where fasting will say, 'There is no entrance through me.' Then he will be questioned by his left side where charity will say, 'There is no entrance through me.' Then he will be questioned by his feet where the good acts of voluntary charity, kindness to relations, and good behavior will say, 'There is no entrance through me.' Then they will say to him, 'Get up.'And he will get up. The sun will appear to him and it will begin to set. Then they will ask, 'This man who was among you, what do you say about him? What is your testimony about him?' The man will say, 'Let me pray.' The angels will say, 'You will pray. Answer our question. What do you think about this man who was among you? What do you say concerning him? What do you testify concerning him?' The deceased will say, I bear witness that Muhammad was the Messenger of God who brought the truth from God.' The deceased will be told, 'According to this you lived, died, and according to this you will be resurrected, if God wills.'

Will Blow the Trumpet

Angel Israfeel[AS] will blow the trumpet when the time for the world to end arrives.[y]

Then a door to Paradise will be opened for him. He will be told, 'This is your place in Paradise and what God has prepared for you. ' At this the desire and happiness of the deceased will increase. His grave will be enlarged 70 arms-length and his grave will be lit up. His body will change to his original form and his spirit will be placed in a bird dangling by the trees of Paradise in a nice breeze." The Prophet, peace be upon him, added, "That is what is meant by the statement of God, 'God will establish in strength those who believe with the Word that stands firm, in this world and in the Hereafter'." He also mentioned the unbeliever and said, "His grave will be compressed, so that his ribs will be crushed together. About this the Qur'an says, 'Verily, for him is a narrow life and We will resurrect him blind on the Day of Resurrection'." Qur'an 20.124[4]

---

[y] God's Messenger (peace be upon him) said, "God created Israfil who has been keeping his feet in line from the day he was created and not raising his glance. Between him and the Lord Who is Blessed and Exalted, there are seventy lights, not one of which he could approach without being burned." (Tirmidhi 5731)

The Prophet (peace be upon him) said: How can I feel happy when the Angel Israfil (the angel appointed to blow the Trumpet on the Day of Judgment) has put his lips to the Trumpet waiting to hear the order to blow the trumpet? This very much distressed his companions, so he told them to seek comfort through reciting "Sufficient for us is God and an excellent Guardian is He". (Tirmidhi 409)

When a third of the night had passed the Prophet (peace be upon him) used to get up and call out: 'O people, remember God; the first call (of the trumpet of Angel Israfil) has sounded; after this comes the second call. It is accompanied by death, and all that it comprise.' I said to the Prophet (peace be upon him): 'O Messenger of God (peace be upon him) I invoke God's peace and blessings upon you copiously; how much time should I earmark for this?' He said: 'As much time as you think proper.' I submitted: 'A quarter of my time?' He said: 'As much you wish; but it would be better for you, if you could devote more time.' I said: 'Half of my time?' He said: 'Whatever you wish; but it would be (still) better for you, if you were to increase it.' Then I said:

Their Role in the Hereafter:

The angels will be very busy on the Day of Judgement.

Will Descend in Rank upon Ranks
The angels will descend rank upon rank on the Day of Judgement, when the court will be established.[z]

Will Carry the Throne of God
Eight angels will carry the throne of God on the Day of Judgement.[aa]

'Two-third of my time?' He said: 'As much you wish; but it would be (still) better for you if you were to increase it.' I said: 'Shall I devote all my time (supplications) to reciting Salat (benediction) on you? He said: 'Then it will take care of all your worries and your sins will be forgiven.' (Tirmidhi 580)

[z] Nay! when the earth is pounded to powder. And your Lord comes and His angels rank upon rank. And Hell that Day is brought (face to face) on that Day will man remember but how will that remembrance profit him? (89:21-23)

The Day the heaven shall be rent asunder with clouds and angels shall be sent down descending (in ranks). That Day the dominion as of right and truth shall be (wholly) for (God) Most Merciful: it will be a day of dire difficulty for the Non-believers. (25:2-26)

(From) the Lord of the heavens and the earth and all between (God) Most Gracious: none shall have power to argue with Him. The Day that the Spirit and the angels will stand forth in ranks none shall speak except any who is permitted by (God) Most Gracious and he will say what is right. That Day will be the sure Reality: therefore whoso will let him take a (straight) Return to his Lord! (78:37-39)

[aa] Then when one Blast is sounded on the Trumpet. And the earth is moved and its mountains and they are crushed to powder at one stroke. On that Day shall the (Great) Event come to pass and the sky will be rent asunder for it will that Day be flimsy and the angels will be on its sides and eight will that Day bear the Throne of your Lord above them. That Day shall you be brought to Judgment: not an act of yours that you hide will be hidden. (69:13-18)

Will Surround the Throne of God
The angels will be surrounding the throne of God on the Day of Judgement.[ab]

Will Escort Humans to the Court
As soon as the Trumpet will be blown on the Day of Judgement, the angels will escort each of us to the court.[ac]

Will Serve as Witness
Whereas one angel will be escorting each of us to the court, another angel will follow us to serve as a witness for our actions in this world.[ad]

Will they wait until God comes to them in canopies of clouds with angels (in His train) and the question is (thus) settled? But to God do all questions go back (for decision). (2:210)

[ab] And you will see the angels surrounding the Throne (Divine) on all sides singing Glory and Praise to their Lord. The Decision between them (at Judgment) will be in (perfect) justice. And the cry (on all sides) will be "Praise be to God the Lord of the Worlds!" (39:75)

[ac] And the Trumpet shall be blown: that will be the Day whereof warning (had been given). And there will come forth every soul: with each will be an (angel) to drive and an (angel) to bear witness. (50:20)

The Prophet said, "You will be gathered (on the Day of Resurrection) and some people will be driven (by the angels) to the left side (and taken to Hell) whereupon I will say as the pious slave (Jesus) said: 'And I was a witness over them while I dwelt amongst them...the All-Mighty, the All Wise.' " (5.117-118) (Bukhari 6.150)

[ad] And the Trumpet shall be blown: that will be the Day whereof warning (had been given). And there will come forth every soul: with each will be an (angel) to drive and an (angel) to bear witness. (It will be said:) "You were heedless of this; now have We removed your veil and sharp is your sight this Day!" And his companion will say: "Here is (his record) ready with me!" (The sentence will be:) "Throw into Hell

Will Escort Humans to Hell and Paradise

After the judgement will be passed, the angels will escort the bad ones to the hell and the good ones to the Paradise.[ae]

Will Salute the Inhabitants of the Paradise

The angels of Paradise will salute the believers upon their arrival in paradise.[af]

---

every contumacious Rejector (of God)! Who forbade what was good transgressed all bounds cast doubts and suspicions; Who set up another god besides God: throw him into a severe Penalty." (50:20-26)

One day He will gather them all together and say to the angels "Was it you that these men used to worship?" They will say "Glory to you! Our (tie) is with you as Protector not with them. Nay but they worshipped the Jinns: most of them believed in them." (34:40-41)

[ae] The Unbelievers will be led to Hell in crowds; until when they arrive there its gates will be opened and its Keepers will say "Did not apostles come to you from among yourselves rehearsing to you the Signs of your Lord and warning you of the meeting of this Day of yours?" The answer will be: "True: but the Decree of Punishment has been proved true against the Unbelievers!" (To them) will be said: "Enter you the gates of Hell to dwell therein: and evil is (this) abode of the arrogant!" And those who feared their Lord will be led to the Garden in crowds: (39:71-73)

[af] And those who feared their Lord will be led to the Garden in crowds: until behold they arrive there; its gates will be opened: and its Keepers will say: "Peace be upon you! Well have you done! Enter you here to dwell therein."

They will say: "Praise be to God Who has truly fulfilled His promise to us and has given us (this) land in heritage: we can dwell in the Garden as we will: how excellent a reward for those who work (righteousness)!"
(39:73-75)

Is then one who does know that that which has been revealed unto these from your Lord is the Truth like one who is blind? It is those who are endued with understanding that receive admonition. Those who fulfill the Covenant of God and fail not in their plighted word. Those who

Will Guard the Hell
The angels of Hell will guard the hell.[ag]

---

join together those things which God has commanded to be joined hold their Lord in awe and fear the terrible reckoning. Those who patiently persevere seeking the countenance their Lord; establish regular prayers; spend out of (the gifts). We have bestowed for their sustenance secretly and openly; and turn off Evil with good: for such there is the final attainment of the (Eternal) Home. Gardens of perpetual bliss: they shall enter there as well as the righteous among their fathers their spouses and their offspring: and angels shall enter unto them from every gate (with the salutation): "Peace unto you for that you persevered in patience! Now how excellent is the final Home!" (13:19-24)

Those for whom the Good (Record) from Us has gone before will be removed far therefrom. Not the slightest sound will they hear of Hell: what their souls desired in that will they dwell. The Great Terror will bring them no grief: but the angels will meet them (with mutual greetings): "This is your Day (the Day) that you were promised." (21:101-104)

[ag] O you who believe! Save yourselves and your families from a Fire whose fuel is Men and Stones over which are (appointed) angels stern (and) severe who flinch not (from executing) the Commands they receive from God but do (precisely) what they are commanded. (66:6)

And what will explain to you what Hell-Fire is? Naught does it permit to endure and naught does it leave alone! Darkening and changing the color of man! Over it are Nineteen. And We have set none but angels as guardians of the Fire; and We have fixed their number only as a trial for Unbelievers in order that the people of the Book may arrive at certainty and the Believers may increase in Faith and that no doubts may be left for the People of the Book and the Believers and that those in whose hearts is a disease and the Unbelievers may say "What symbol does God intend by this?" Thus does God leave to stray whom He pleases and guide whom He pleases; and none can know the forces of the Lord except He and this is no other than a warning to mankind. (74:27-31)

The Sinners will be in the Punishment of Hell to dwell therein (for aye): Nowise will the (punishment) be lightened for them and in despair will they be there overwhelmed. Nowise shall We be unjust to them: but it is they who have been unjust themselves. They will cry: "O

Summary:

The angels, having no will of their own, only execute the commands of God. They are executing His commands in this world and will be doing the same in the Hereafter. In this world they sustain the throne of God, are busy glorifying Him all the time, and serve as witness to the Oneness of God and the truthfulness of the Prophets. They serve as His messengers to humans, guard them, record their deeds, test their character, and repel evil from them. They help the prophets and the believers, comfort and implore forgiveness for the believers, and send peace and blessing to the believers and Prophet Muhammad^{SAW}. They curse and impose final punishment on the rejecters of the prophets. They take the soul away at the time of death, question the dead, and will blow the trumpet that will mark the end of this world. In the Hereafter they will descend carrying and surrounding the throne of God. They will escort the humans to

---

Malik! would that your Lord put and end to us!" He will say "Nay but you shall abide!" (43:74-77)

For those who reject their Lord (and Cherisher) is the Penalty of Hell: and evil is (such) destination. When they are cast therein they will hear the (terrible) drawing in of its breath even as it blazes forth. Almost bursting with fury: every time a Group is cast therein its Keepers will ask "Did no Warner come to you?" They will say: "Yes indeed: a Warner did come to us but we rejected him and said `God never sent down any (Message): you are in nothing but an egregious delusion!" They will further say: "Had we but listened or used our intelligence we should not (now) be among the Companions of the Blazing Fire!" They will then confess their sins: but far will be (Forgiveness) from the Companions of the Blazing Fire! (67:6-11)

Those in the Fire will say to the Keepers of Hell: "Pray to your Lord to lighten us the Penalty for a Day (at least)!" They will say: "Did there not come to you your apostles with Clear Signs?" They will say "Yes." They will reply "Then pray (as you like) but the Prayer of those without Faith is nothing but (futile wandering) in (mazes of) error!" (40:49-50)

God's Apostle (peace be upon him) said: The Hell would be brought on that day (the Day of Judgment) with seventy bridles and every bridle would be controlled by seventy angels. (Muslim 6810)

the court and serve as witness for their actions in this world. They will escort the bad ones to the Hell and lead the good ones to the Paradise. The angel of Paradise will salute the good ones at the door of Paradise and angels of the Hell will guard those in the Hell.

Chapter 23
The Famous Angels

The Holy Quran and Prophet Muhammad[SAW] mention some angels by name and some by function. In this chapter we will describe them in detail.

Gabriel (Jibraeel[AS]) (*Ar-Rooh-ul-Ameen*):
Angel Gabriel (Jibraeel[AS]) has been mentioned by name in the Holy Quran.[a] According to most of the scholars[1,2,3], he has also been called the Spirit (*Ar-Rooh*) (and '*Rooh*'),[b] the Trustworthy

---

[a] Say: Whoever is an enemy to Gabriel for he brings down the (revelation) to your heart by God's will a confirmation of what went before and guidance and glad tidings for those who believe. Whoever is an enemy to God and His angels and apostles to Gabriel and Michael Lo! God is an enemy to those who reject faith. (2:97-98)

[b] The angels and the Spirit (*Ar-Rooh*) ascend unto Him in a Day the measure whereof is (as) fifty thousand years: (70:4)

The Day that the Spirit (*Ar-Rooh*) and the angels will stand forth in ranks none shall speak except any who is permitted by (God) Most Gracious and he will say what is right. (78:38)

Therein come down the angels and the Spirit (*Ar-Rooh*) by God's permission on every errand (97:4)

With it came down the Spirit of Faith and Truth (*Ar-Rooh-ul-Ameen*). (26:193)

Relate in the Book (the story of) Mary when she withdrew from her family to a place in the East. She placed a screen (to screen herself) from them: then We sent to her Our angel (*Rooh*) and he appeared before her as a man in all respects. She said: "I seek refuge from you to (God) Most Gracious: (come not near) if you does fear God." He said: "Nay I am only a messenger from your Lord (to announce) to you the gift of a holy son." She said: "How shall I have a son seeing that no man has touched me and I am not unchaste?" He said: "So (it will be): your Lord says `That is easy for Me: and (We wish) to appoint him as a

Spirit (*Rooh-ul-Ameen*), and the Holy Spirit (*Rooh-ul-Quds*).[c] Angel Gabriel (Jibraeel[AS]) was responsible for bringing the message to the Prophets.[c] He also provided strength to Prophet Jesus (Isa[AS]).[d] He also descends every year in the Night

---

Sign unto men and a Mercy from Us': it is a matter (so) decreed." (19:16-21)

[c] Verily this is the word of a most honorable Messenger, endued with Power with rank before the Lord of the Throne. With authority there, (and) faithful to his trust. And (O people!) your companion is not one possessed. And without doubt he saw him in the clear horizon. (81:19-23)

Verily this is a Revelation from the Lord of the Worlds. With it came down the Spirit of Faith and Truth (*Ar-Rooh-ul-Ameen*). To your heart and mind that you may admonish. In the perspicuous Arabic tongue. Without doubt it is (announced) in the mystic Books of former peoples. (26:192-196)

When We substitute one revelation for another and God knows best what He reveals (in stages) they say "You art but a forger": but most of them understand not. Say the Holy Spirit (*Rooh-al-Quds*) has brought the revelation from your Lord in truth in order to strengthen those who believe and as a guide and Glad Tidings to Muslims. (16:101-102)

And thus have We inspired in you (Muhammad) a Spirit (*Rooh*) of Our command. You knew not what the Scripture was, nor what the Faith. But We have made it a light whereby We guide whom We will of Our bondmen. And lo! you verily do guide unto a right path. The path of God, unto Whom belongs whatsoever is in the heavens and whatsoever is in the earth. Do not all things reach God at last? (42:52-53) MP

[d] Those apostles We endowed with gifts some above others: to one of them God spoke; others He raised to degrees (of honor); to Jesus the son of Mary We gave clear (Signs) and strengthened him with the Holy Spirit (*Rooh-al-Quds*). If God had so willed succeeding generations would not have fought among each other after clear (Signs) had come to them but they (chose) to wrangle some believing and others rejecting. If God had so willed they would not have fought each other; but God fulfills His plan. (2:253)

We gave Moses the Book and followed him up with a succession of Apostles; We gave Jesus the son of Mary clear (Signs) and strengthened him with the Holy Spirit (*Rooh-al-Quds*). Is it that

of Power in the month of Ramadhan.ᵉ He is probably the most powerful angel and is endued with wisdom.ᶠ Most of the angels

---

whenever there comes to you an Apostle with what you yourselves desire not you are puffed up with pride? Some you called impostors and others you slay! (2:87)

Then will God say: "O Jesus the son of Mary! recount my favor to you and to your mother. Behold! I strengthened you with the Holy Spirit (*Rooh-al-Quds*) so that you did speak to the people in childhood and in maturity. Behold! I taught you the Book and Wisdom the Law and the Gospel. And behold! you make out of clay as it were the figure of a bird by My leave and you breath into it and it becomes a bird by My leave and you heal those born blind and the lepers by My leave. And behold! You bring forth the dead by My leave. And behold! I did restrain the Children of Israel from (violence to) you when you did show them the Clear Signs and the unbelievers among them said: `This is nothing but evident magic'. (5:110)

ᵉ We have indeed revealed this (Message) in the night of Power. And what will explain to you what the Night of Power is? The Night of Power is better than a thousand Months. Therein come down the angels and the Spirit by God's permission on every errand. Peace!... This until the rise of Morn! (97:1-5)

God's Messenger (peace be upon him) said that when Laylat al-Qadr comes, Gabriel descends with a company of angels who invoke blessings on ever who is standing or sitting and remembering God, who is Great and Glorious. Then when their festival day comes, i.e. the day when they break their fast, God speaks proudly of them to His angels saying, "My angels, what is the reward of a hired servant who has fully accomplished his work?" They reply, "Our Lord, his reward is that he should be paid his wage in full." He says, "My angels, My male and female servants have fulfilled what I have made obligatory for them, and then have come out raising their voices in supplication. By My might, glory, honour, high dignity and exalted station, I shall certainly answer them." Then He says, "Return, for I have forgiven you and changed your evil deeds into good deeds." He said that they then returned having received forgiveness. (Al-Tirmidhi:2096)

ᶠ It is no less than inspiration sent down to him. He was taught by one mighty in Power. Endued with Wisdom: For he appeared (in stately form), (53:4-6)

have two, three, or four pairs of wings,^g but Angel Gabriel (Jibraeel^{AS}) has six hundred wings.^h

Michael (Mikaeel^{AS}):

Angel Michael (Mikaeel^{AS}) has also been mentioned by name in the Holy Quran.ⁱ Statements of Prophet Muhammad^{SAW} suggest that he is also one of the highest ranking angel.^j According to

---

Verily this is the word of a most honorable Messenger, endued with Power with rank before the Lord of the Throne. With authority there, (and) faithful to his trust. And (O people!) your companion is not one possessed. And without doubt he saw him in the clear horizon. (81:19-23)

^g Praise be to God Who created (out of nothing) the heavens and the earth Who made the angels messengers with wings two or three or four (Pairs): He adds to Creation as He pleases: for God has power over all things. (35:1)

^h Prophet Muhammad once saw the Angel Gabriel (Jibraeel^{AS}) with six hundred wings. (Bukhari, Muslim, Tirmidhi)[4]

Prophet Muhammad had seen Angel Gabriel (Jibraeel^{AS}) twice in his real shape: he had six hundred wings and had covered the whole horizon. (Tirmidhi)[5]

ⁱ Whoever is an enemy to God and His angels and apostles to Angels Gabriel (Jibraeel^{AS}) and Michael (Mikaeel^{AS}). Lo! God is an enemy to those who reject faith. (2:98)

^j 'Abdullah said, "Whenever we prayed behind the Prophet we used to recite (in sitting) 'Peace be on Gabriel, Michael, peace be on so and so.' (Bukhari 1.794, 8.249)

The Prophet said, "Last night I saw (in a dream) two men coming to me. One of them said, "The person who kindles the fire is Malik, the gate-keeper of the (Hell) Fire, and I am Gabriel, and this is Michael." (Bukhari 4.459 also 2.468)

When he (the Apostle of God) got up at night he would commence his prayer with these words: O God, Lord of Gabriel, and Michael, and Israfeel, the Creator of the heavens and the earth, Who knows the

Yousuf Islahi[6], Michael (Mikaeel[AS]) is responsible for arranging for rain and food. According to Encyclopaedia Britannica, Michael (Mikaeel[AS]) in Islam 'is the controller of the forces of nature who – with 1,000 assistants called *karubiyun*, or cherubim – provides men with both food and knowledge.[7] He is probably responsible for providing spiritual and physical nourishment.

Israfeel[AS]:

Israfeel[AS] is responsible for blowing the Trumpet that will mark the end of this world. Although he has not been mentioned by name in the Holy Quran, his name appears in the statements of Prophet Muhammad[SAW]. Ever since he has been created, he has been keeping his feet in line and not raising his glance. He has put his lips to the Trumpet waiting to hear the order to blow the trumpet? Angel Gabriel (Jibraeel[AS]) is sitting on his right and Angel Michael (Mikaeel[AS]) on his left.[k] Statements of Prophet Muhammad[SAW] suggest that he is also one the high ranking angels.[l]

---

unseen and the seen; Thou decides among Thy servants concerning their difference. Guide me with Thy permission in the divergent views (which the people) hold about Truth, for it is Thou Who guides whom You wilt to the Straight Path. (Muslim 1694)

[k] God's Messenger (peace be upon him) said, "God created Israfil who has been keeping his feet in line from the day he was created and not raising his glance. Between him and the Lord Who is Blessed and Exalted, there are seventy lights, not one of which he could approach without being burned." Tirmidhi transmitted it and called it sahih. (Tirmidhi 5731)

[l] Abu al-Malih (whose name was 'Aamr ibn Usamah)'s father had prayed the two rak'at of the dawn [before salatul fajr] and the Prophet sallGodu alehi wasallam was praying the two rak'at close to him, and he heard the Prophet say, while sitting:

'O God, Lord of Jibrail, Israfeel, Mikail, and Muhammad, the Prophet, I seek refuge in Thee from the Fire,'"...three times. (Fiqh-us-Sunnah)

The Prophet (peace be upon him) said: How can I feel happy when the Angel Israfil (the angel appointed to blow the Trumpet on the Day of

Izrael[AS] (The Angel of Death, *Malak-al-Mawt*):

Izrael[AS] is not mentioned by name, but by his function in the Holy Quran.[m] He is responsible for taking soul of all the living souls at the time of death.[9] However, he does not do this job alone.[n] He is assigned quite a few angels to assist him.

Judgment) has put his lips to the Trumpet waiting to hear the order to blow the trumpet? This very much distressed his companions, so he told them to seek comfort through reciting "Sufficient for us is God and an excellent Guardian is He". (Tirmidhi 409)

When a third of the night had passed the Prophet (peace be upon him) used to get up and call out: 'O people, remember God; the first call (of the trumpet of Angel Israfil) has sounded; after this comes the second call. It is accompanied by death, and all that it comprise. (Tirmidhi 580)

The Apostle of God gave the description of the holder of the Trumpet, and he said that by his right side is Angel Gabriel (Jibraeel[AS]) and by his left side is Angel Michael (Mikaeel [AS]).[8] (Mishkat Chapter XL, Section 4, 644w)

The trumpet shall be sounded when behold! From the sepulchers (men) will rush forth to their Lord! (36:51)

The Day that the Trumpet shall be sounded and you shall come forth in crowds; (78:18)

[m] Say: "The Angel of Death, put in charge of you, will (duly) take your souls. Then shall you be brought back to your Lord," (32:11)

[n] He is the Irresistible (watching) from above over his worshippers and He sets guardians over you. At length when death approaches one of you Our angels take his soul and they never fail in their duty. (6:61)

By the (angels) who tear out (the souls of the wicked) with violence. By those who gently draw out (the souls of the blessed). (79:1-2)

If you could see, when the angels take souls of the unbelievers (at death). (How) they smite their faces and their backs, (saying): "Taste the Penalty of the blazing fire. (8:50)

But how (will it be) when the angels take their souls at death, and smite their faces and their backs. (47:27)

Malik:

Angel Malik is mentioned by name in the Holy Quran.° He is the guardian of Hell. He will probably be in charge of making sure no one runs away from hell and gets proper punishment.

How the wicked (do fare) in the flood of confusion at death - the angels stretch forth their hands, (saying), "Yield up your souls. This day shall you receive your reward - a penalty of shame, for that you used to tell lies against God, and scornfully to reject of His Signs!" (6:93)

Those whose lives the angels take in a state of wrongdoing to their souls. Then would they offer submission (with the pretense), 'We did no evil (knowingly)." (The angels will reply), "Nay, but verily God knows all that you did; so enter the gates of Hell, to dwell therein. Thus evil indeed is the abode of the arrogant." (16:28-29)

When angels take the souls of those who die in sin against their souls they say: "In what (plight) were you?" They reply: "Weak and oppressed were we in the earth." They say: "Was not the earth of God spacious enough for you to move yourselves away (from evil)?" Such men will find their abode in Hell what an evil refuge! (4:97)

Who is more unjust than one who invents a lie against God or rejects his signs? For such their portion appointed must reach them from the Book (of decrees); until when Our messengers (of death) arrive and take their souls they say: "where are the things that you used to invoke besides God?" They will reply "they have left us in the lurch" and they will bear witness against themselves that they had rejected God. He will say: "enter you in the company of the peoples who passed away before you men and Jinns into the fire. (7:37-38)

Those whose lives the angels take in a state of purity, saying (to them), "Peace be on you, enter you the Garden, because of (the good) which you did (in the world). (16:32)

° The Sinners will be in the Punishment of Hell to dwell therein (for aye): Nowise will the (punishment) be lightened for them and in despair will they be there overwhelmed. Nowise shall We be unjust to them: but it is they who have been unjust themselves. They will cry: "O Malik! would that your Lord put and end to us!" He will say "Nay but you shall abide!" (43:74-77)

Haroot and Maroot:

Haroot and Maroot were two angels sent to the Children of Israeel[p] to test them while they were living in captivity in Babylon[10]:

Guardian Angels (*Kiraman Katebeen*) (Recorders of Deeds):

Guardian Angels called *Kiraman Katebeen* is not the proper name of any angel. This is a class of angels assigned to each person to guard him and record his deeds.[q]

The Prophet said, "Last night I saw (in a dream) two men coming to me. One of them said, "The person who kindles the fire is Malik, the gate-keeper of the (Hell) Fire, and I am Gabriel, and this is Michael." (Bukhari 4.459 also 2.468)

[p] They followed what the evil ones gave out (falsely) against the power of Solomon; the blasphemers were not Solomon but the evil ones teaching men magic and such things as came down at Babylon to the angels Haroot and Maroot. But neither of these taught anyone (such things) without saying: "We are only for trial so do not blaspheme." They learned from them the means to sow discord between man and wife. But they could not thus harm anyone except by God's permission. And they learned what harmed them not what profited them. And they knew that the buyers of (magic) would have no share in the happiness of the Hereafter. And vile was the price for which they did sell their souls if they but knew! (2:102)

[q] Behold two (guardian angels) appointed to learn (his doings) learn (and note them) one sitting on the right and one on the left. Not a word does he utter but there is a sentinel by him ready (to note it). (50:17-18)

For each (such person) there are (angels) in succession before and behind him: they guard him by command of God. Verily never will God change the condition of a people until they change it themselves (with their own souls). But when (once) God wills a people's punishment there can be no turning it back nor will they find besides Him any to protect. (13:11)

But verily over you (are appointed angels) to protect you – Kind and Honorable writing down (your deeds). They know (and understand) all that you do. (82:10-12)

Or do they think that We hear not their secrets and their private

Munkar Nakeer (The Two Questioning Angels):

Munkar Nakeer is not the proper name of any angel. This is a class of angels responsible for questioning the dead in the grave.[r]

counsels? Indeed (We do), and Our Messengers are by them, to record.' (43:80)

[r] Hanbal said, "I heard Abu Abdallah saying, 'We believe in the punishment of the grave, in Munkar and Nakir (the two questioning angels), and that the deceased will be questioned in their graves.' The Qur'an states that 'God will establish in strength those who believe in the Word, that stands firm in this world and in the Hereafter,' Qur'an 14.27 that is, in the grave."[11, 12]

Prophet Muhammad[SAW] said, 'When a human is laid in his grave and his companions return and he hears their footsteps, two angels will come to him and make him sit and ask him, "What did you say about this man, Muhammad, may peace be upon him?" He will say, "I testify that he is God's servant and His Messenger." Then it will be said to him, "Look at your place in Hell-Fire. God has exchanged for you a place in Paradise instead of it".' The Prophet, peace be upon him, added, 'The dead person will see both his places. As for a non-believer or a hypocrite, he will respond to the angels, "I do not know, but I used to say what the people used to say ! " It will be said to him, "Neither did you know nor did you seek guidance from those who had knowledge." Then he will be hit with an iron hammer between his two ears, and he will cry and that cry will be heard by all except human beings and jinns'." (Bukhari and Muslim)[13]

Prophet Muhammad[SAW] said, 'When a Muslim is questioned in his grave, he bears witness that there is no god but God, and that Muhammad is the Messenger of God.' According to one report, the verse, 'God will establish in strength those who believe with the Word, that stands firm in this world and in the Hereafter' (Qur'an 14.27) was revealed concerning the punishment of the grave. The deceased will be asked, 'Who is your Lord?' He will say, 'God is my Lord and Muhammad is my Prophet.' That is what is meant by the statement of God, 'God will make firm those who believe with a firm statement in this life and in the hereafter'." (Al-Bukhari, Muslim, and Sunan)[14]

Prophet Muhammad[SAW] said, "When a deceased person is laid in his grave, he hears the sound of the footsteps of people as they go away. If he is a believer, the prayer will stand by his head, the fasting will be to his right, alms to his left, and all other good deeds of charity, kindness to relations, and good behavior will be by his feet. The deceased will

Summary:

The Holy Quran and the statements of Prophet Muhammad[SAW] mention the following angels by name or function:

> Angel Gabriel (Jibraeel[AS]), who brought messages to the Prophets and others and descends on the Night of Power in the month of Ramadhan;

---

be questioned by the angels at his head. The prayer will say, 'There is no entrance through me.' Then he will be questioned by his right side where fasting will say, 'There is no entrance through me.' Then he will be questioned by his left side where charity will say, 'There is no entrance through me.' Then he will be questioned by his feet where the good acts of voluntary charity, kindness to relations, and good behavior will say, 'There is no entrance through me.' Then they will say to him, 'Get up. 'And he will get up. The sun will appear to him and it will begin to set. Then they will ask, 'This man who was among you, what do you say about him? What is your testimony about him?' The man will say, 'Let me pray.' The angels will say, 'You will pray. Answer our question. What do you think about this man who was among you? What do you say concerning him? What do you testify concerning him?' The deceased will say, I bear witness that Muhammad was the Messenger of God who brought the truth from God.' The deceased will be told, 'According to this you lived, died, and according to this you will be resurrected, if God wills.'

Then a door to Paradise will be opened for him. He will be told, 'This is your place in Paradise and what God has prepared for you. ' At this the desire and happiness of the deceased will increase. His grave will be enlarged 70 arms-length and his grave will be lit up. His body will change to his original form and his spirit will be placed in a bird dangling by the trees of Paradise in a nice breeze." The Prophet, peace be upon him, added, "That is what is meant by the statement of God, 'God will establish in strength those who believe with the Word that stands firm, in this world and in the Hereafter'." He also mentioned the unbeliever and said, "His grave will be compressed, so that his ribs will be crushed together. About this the Qur'an says, 'Verily, for him is a narrow life and We will resurrect him blind on the Day of Resurrection'." Qur'an 20.124[15]

Angel Michael (Mikaeel[AS]), who is the controller of the forces of nature and provides men with both food and knowledge;

Israfeel[AS], who is waiting to blow the Trumpet to mark the end of the world;

Izraeel[AS], who is the angel of death;

Malik, who is the guardian of Hell;

Haroot and Maroot, who were sent to the Children of Israeel during their captivity in Babylon;

Guardian Angels (*Kiraman Katebeen*), the two angels who are assigned to each person to guard him and record his deeds; and

Munkir Nakeer, the two angels assigned to question the dead in the grave.

Angel Gabriel (Jibraeel[AS]), Angel Michael (Mikaeel[AS]), and Angel Israfeel[AS] seem to be the top ranking angels[16].

Chapter 24
The Angels and the Humans

In this chapter we will discuss the relationship and the difference between the angels and the humans.

Different Origin and State:
The angels and humans have different origin. The angels are made from photons and the humans are made from cells. Due to the difference in their origin, the angels exhibit the characteristics of photons and the humans exhibit the characteristics of the cells. Due to their cellular origin, the humans are neither stiff like iron, nor fluid like water. They have a definite size and shape, but also possess some flexibility in movement. The angels, having originated from photons, possess neither mass, nor volume. Their characteristics should be similar to the electromagnetic wave. As such their shape should be that of a wave. Their size (length of wave) will be dictated by the frequency of the wave. The angels are also invisible and imperceptible. Humans do not possess these characteristics. Depending upon their energy, the angels can penetrate the human body.

Life Span:
Whereas humans have a limited life span, the angels will live until the end of the universe.

Pro-creation:
Since humans have a limited life span, they pro-create to preserve their species. Since the angels will live until the end of the Universe, they do not need to procreate.

Gender:
Whereas humans have males and females, the angels do not have any gender.

Free Will:
The humans have been given a free will.[a] The angels are not given any free will. They only execute God's commands.[b]

Created before Humans:
Our study shows that, whereas humans appeared within last one or two million years, the angels were created within one million years after the creation of the universe. When God announced the creation of Adam[AS], angels were already in existence.[c]

---

[a] By the Soul and the proportion and order Given to it. And its enlightenment as to its wrong and its right. Truly he succeeds that purifies it. And he fails that corrupts it! (91:7-10)

[b] And by those who glide along (on errands of mercy). Then press forward as in a race. Then arrange to do (the commands of their Lord) (79:3-5)

O you who believe! Save yourselves and your families from a Fire whose fuel is Men and Stones over which are (appointed) angels stern (and) severe who flinch not (from executing) the Commands they receive from God but do (precisely) what they are commanded. (66:6)

And to God does obeisance all that is in the heavens and on the earth whether moving (living) creatures or the angels: for none are arrogant (before their Lord). They all revere their Lord high above them and they do all that they are commanded. (16:49-50)

[c] Behold thy Lord said to the angels: "I will create a vicegerent on the earth." They said "Wilt thou place therein one who will make mischief therein and shed blood? Whilst we do celebrate Thy praises and glorify Thy holy (name)?" He said: "I know what ye know not." (2:30)

Behold, your Lord said to the angels: " I am about to create man from clay. When I have fashioned him (in due proportion) and breathed into him My spirit, fall you down in obeisance unto him." So the angels prostrated themselves, all of them together. Not so Iblees. He was haughty, and he became one of those who reject Faith. (38:71-74)

Inferior to Humans:
Humans are superior to angels. It was the knowledge God gave to Adam^AS that made humans superior to angels.^d Humans are the vicegerents of God on this earth.^e They are the best of the creatures.^f Everything in the heaven and the earth is subjected to them.^g

Influence on Humans:
The following statement of Prophet Muhammad^SAW suggests that the angels influence humans by persuading them to do good deeds.^h

---

^d And He taught Adam the nature of all things; then He placed them before the angels and said: "Tell Me the nature of these if you are right."

They said: "Glory to You of knowledge we have none save that You have taught us: in truth it is You who art perfect in knowledge and wisdom."

He said: "O Adam! tell them their natures." When he had told them God said: "Did I not tell you that I know the secrets of heaven and the earth and I know what you reveal and what you conceal?"

And behold We said to the angels: "Bow down to Adam"; and they bowed down not so Iblees he refused and was haughty he was of those who reject Faith. (2:31-34)

^e Behold, Your Lord said to the angels: "I will create a vicegerent on the earth." (2:30)

^f We have indeed created human being in the best of moulds. (95:4)

-- And (He) has given you shape, and made your shapes beautiful – (40:64, 64:3)

^g Do you not see that God has subjected to your (use) all the things in the heavens and on the earth, and has made his bounties flow to you in exceeding measure, (both) seen and unseen. (31:20)

^h Every human being has two houses in his heart. In one house lives an angel and in the other house lives Satan (evil Jinn). The angel persuades him to do good deeds and the Satan persuades him to do bad

Communication:

We have already discussed in Chapter 20 (The Intellectual Ability of the Angels) that the angels can communicate with humans in general after assuming human form and can speaks directly with God and the prophets. Humans cannot initiate communication with the angels at will. The angels, on the other hand, communicate with human beings through thoughts and give them ideas and suggestions.[i] God does not speak directly to humans. The only exception was Prophet Moses (Moosa[AS]), with whom he talked directly, but behind a veil.[j]

---

deeds. When he is busy remembering God, the Satan backs off. When he is not busy in remembrance of God, the Satan persuades him to do bad deeds.[1]

[i] Every human being has two houses in his heart. In one house lives an angel and in the other house lives Satan (evil Jinn). The angel persuades him to do good deeds and the Satan persuades him to do bad deeds. When he is busy remembering God, the Satan backs off. When he is not busy in remembrance of God, the Satan persuades him to do bad deeds.[2]

[j] It is not fitting for a man that God should speak to him except by inspiration or from behind a veil or by the sending of a Messenger to reveal with God's permission what God wills: for He is Most High Most Wise. (42:51)
---- and to Moses (Moosa) God spoke direct. (4:164)

(God) said: "O Moses (Moosa)! I have chosen you above (other) men by the mission I (have given you) and the words I (have spoken to you): take then the (revelation) which I give you and be of those who give thanks." (7:143)
Those apostles We endowed with gifts some above others: to one of them God spoke; others He raised to degrees (of honor); to Jesus the son of Mary We gave clear (Signs) and strengthened him with the Holy Spirit. (2:253)

Speed:
Compared to the speed of humans, which is only 3 to 15 miles per hour, the angels move at the speed of light (670 milion miles per hour). Even rocket, which so far is the fastest mode of transportation developed by humans, can only reach a speed of 25,000 miles per hour.[3]

Space Adventure:
Whereas humans have only traveled to the moon[4], the angels can roam throughout the universe at the speed of light.

Transformation:
The angels have the ability to acquire human form. Human beings do not have any capability to change their state.

Summary:
Compared to humans, who possess mass and occupy space, the angels have no mass and do not occupy any space. They are invisible and imperceptible to humans. They could be highly penetrative to human body. They travel in a straight line at the speed of light. Humans have to struggle to walk straight. The angels were probably created within million years after the creation of the universe and will live until the end of the universe. Humans have been on this planet for less one or two million years. The angels have no free will. They do not procreate and have no gender. Humans have a free will. They procreate and have gender. The angels directly communicate with God. Except Prophet Moses (Moosa[AS]), even the prophets had no direct communication with God. The angels also have the ability to initiate communication with humans. The humans, even the prophets, cannot initiate communication with them. The angels can transform into human form, but are inferior to humans.

Chapter 25
Summary

The analysis of the Quranic statements in view of current scientific understanding and the statements of Prophet Muhammad^{SAW} suggests that the angels are made from photons. Photons have zero mass, travel at the speed of light, do not occupy any space, and possess energy and power. They are probably behind the electromagnetic force or could be the force themselves. This view is supported by the role electromagnetic force plays in modern day communication equipment and electronic gadgets, which basically involve communication and execution of command.

There are many types of angels; each type has a particular power. The power of these angels will depend upon the frequency of the electromagnetic wave their photon is part of. The angels made from photons corresponding to the frequency of Cosmic rays will be most powerful and the angels made from photons corresponding to the frequency of Radio waves will be the least powerful among all the angels.

According to another interpretation (Appendix C), the angels could be behind the three fundamental forces of nature: electromagnetic, nuclear, and gravitational forces. The gravitational force keeps us firmly planted on the earth and keeps the moon in orbit around the earth and the earth and other planets in orbit around the sun. It is responsible for forming most of the structures in the universe, including galaxies, stars, and planets. The nuclear force brings hydrogen atoms together to form helium that results in the creation of photons in the sun and all the stars. The electromagnetic force in turn drive almost all the activities on the earth. Just as the photons are the force particles associated with the electromagnetic forces, gluons and gravitons are associated with the nuclear, and the gravitational forces, respectively. The three types of angels will then correspond to the three forces of nature. Since we know more about electromagnetic forces and less about nuclear and magnetic forces, the rest of the discussion was based on the electromagnetic forces. The same will be applicable to the other two forces.

The physical characteristics of the angels should be dictated by the physical characteristics of the electromagnetic forces. Many of these characteristics are confirmed by the statements made in the Holy Quran and by Prophet Muhammad^{SAW}. They should be shaped in the form of wave and the size should be dictated by the frequency of the wave they correspond to. They form straight line and glide throughout the universe at the speed of light. Their energy, power, and penetrative ability will depend upon the frequency of the photons they are made from. Higher the frequency, higher will be the energy, power, and penetrative ability.

The angels are living beings. The Quranic statements and our scientific understanding of their nature suggests that all the angels could have been born about a million years after the creation of the universe and will not die until the end of the universe. Humans have only been on this planet for less than one or two million years. They have no gender and do not procreate. The probably consume photons to do purposeful work.

The angels are intellectual beings. The angels, like human beings, have the power of observation and intelligence. They are invisible and imperceptible to humans. They have the ability to transform themselves into human form. They communicate with humans through their thought process and with prophets. They can also converse directly with human beings after acquiring human form. They directly communicate with God. Except Prophet Moses (Moosa^{AS}), even the prophets had no direct communication with God. The angels also have the ability to initiate communication with humans. The humans, even the prophets, cannot initiate communication with them. They can transform into human form, but are inferior to humans. They also possess knowledge, but it is not at par with that of humans.

The angels believe in and testify the Oneness of God and the truthfulness of all the Prophets. Since they do not have a free will, there will be no reward or punishment for them on the day of Judgement. They only execute the command of God and only serve Him. They are busy executing His command in this world and will be busy doing the same in the Hereafter. In this world, they sustain the throne of God and are busy glorifying Him. They serve as God's messengers to humans, guard them, record their deeds, test their character, and repel evil from them. They help the prophets and the believers, comfort and implore forgiveness for the believers, and send peace and blessing to the believers and Prophet Muhammad[SAW]. They curse and impose final punishment on the rejecters of the prophets. They take the soul away at the time of death, question the dead, and will blow the trumpet that will mark the end of this world. In the Hereafter, they will descend carrying and surrounding the throne of God. They will escort the humans to the court and serve as witness for their actions in this world. They will escort the bad ones to the Hell and lead the good ones to the Paradise. They will salute the good ones at the door of Paradise and guard those in the Hell.

Section IV

DEMONS

Chapter 26
The Demons

The term demon, according to Encyclopaedia Britannica[1], is derived from the Greek word *daimon,* which means a 'supernatural being' or 'spirit.' The term originally meant a spiritual being that influenced a person's character. In Western religions, however, the term is commonly associated with an evil or malevolent spirit. They tempt humans to commit sin and place obstacles for them in developing relationship with God. They are believed to cause various types of calamities. They are believed to posses people afflicted with mental ailment. They were believed to inhabit waterless water lands.[1] The Holy Bible mentions four instances in which Jesus cast out devil or unclean spirits from men.[2-5]

Islam classifies spiritual beings into angels (*malaikah*) and the Jinns.[1] As discussed in Section III, the angels are always good because they do not have a free will. The Jinns, as discussed in Section I, could be good or bad because they have free will. The Holy Quran calls the bad Jinns '*shayateen*' (evils). Based on the characteristics described earlier, the Western term of demons is equivalent to the Quranic term '*shayateen*' (evils). Demons are those Jinns who follow Satan. This will include Satan's children, his tribe, and the bad Jinns. Satan is their Godfather. They are doing his bidding.

The Characteristics and the Ability of the Demons:
Since demons are the evil Jinns, they will possess all the physical and biological characteristics of the Jinns. They are probably made from carbon dioxide gases. They are invisible, imperceptible, and penetrative. It gives them great power and flexibility in size and shape. They can travel at an average speed of about 850 miles per hour, and can fathom space up to an altitude of about 60 to 70 miles. They have the ability to acquire human and other animal forms.

They have the power of observation, intelligence, free

will, conscience, and guidance. They are also created to worship God and are expected to believe in the same things the human being is expected to believe in. They will suffer post-death punishment, will be resurrected, will be accountable for their deeds, and will be rewarded accordingly on the Day of Judgment. They are inferior to humans. They can see the humans and listen to their conversation, but the human being cannot see them or listen to their conversation. They can also see and hear the angels within the altitude of 60 to 70 miles.

The Companion Demon:
Every human being, according to the statements of Prophet Muhammad^{SAW}, has a companion demon (satan or evil Jinn) with him.[a] Since the demons are made form carbon dioxide, we expect them to live in carbon dioxide rich environment. Although the heart has four chambers, two chambers (right atrium and right ventricle) have carbon dioxide rich blood and two chambers (left atrium and left ventricle) have oxygen rich blood. Probably the demon lives in the carbon dioxide rich chambers.

According to another statement of Prophet

---

[a] Every human being has two houses in his heart. In one house lives an angel and in the other house lives satan (evil Jinn). The angel persuades him to do good deeds and the satan persuades him to do bad deeds. When he is busy remembering God, the satan backs off. When he is not busy in remembrance of God, the satan persuades him to do bad deeds. (quoted from Maarif-ul-Quran and Tafseer-e-Mazhari)[6]

There is none amongst you with whom is not attached from amongst the jinn (devil). --- Yes (even with me), but God helps me against him and so I am safe from his hand and he does not command me but for good. (Muslim: 6757, 6758)

(Devil) is attached to everyone, ---- (even with me), but my Lord has helped me against him and as such I am absolutely safe from his mischief. (Muslim: 6759)

Muhammad^SAW, this companionship starts right after the birth.[b] We have already discussed under Section II that, because of his limitations, Satan cannot be everywhere. Probably it is the companion demon who makes the first contact.

The touch of the demon at the moment of baby's birth coincides with the physiological change that takes place in the baby's organs at the time of his birth. Humans, like any other terrestrial animal, constantly breathe to stay alive. Breathing is a result of constant expansion and contraction of lungs. When the lungs expand, air is inhaled into the lungs and when they contract, air is exhaled out of the lungs. During the inhalation, the blood in the lungs absorbs oxygen from air and returns carbon dioxide to air. The inhaled air contains 21 percent oxygen and 0.03 percent carbon dioxide and the exhaled air contains 15.3% oxygen and 3.7 percent carbon dioxide.[7] The oxygen-rich blood in the lungs is sucked into the heart (left atrium and left ventricle) from where it is pumped to the body. The carbon dioxide rich blood from the body is sucked into the heart (right atrium and right ventricle) and then pumped back to the lungs. When the baby is inside the womb of the mother, he does not breathe. His lungs are in the collapsed state. The carbon dioxide in baby's blood is exchanged by oxygen in mother's blood. When the baby is born, he loses contact with the mother, and needs to breathe to supply oxygen to the blood. As soon as he cries, his lungs expand and baby starts breathing on his own.[8]

Since demons are made from carbon dioxide, the statements suggest that the companion demon enters the baby's

---

[b] There is none born among the off-spring of Adam, but Satan touches it. A child therefore, cries loudly at the time of birth because of the touch of Satan, except Mary and her child. (Bukhari: 4.641, 6.71)

When any human being is born, Satan touches him at both sides of the body with his two fingers, except Jesus, the son of Mary, whom Satan tried to touch but failed, for he touched the placenta-cover instead. (Bukhari: 4.506)

God's Messenger (peace be upon him) said: The crying of the child (starts) when the satan begins to prick him. (Muslim: 5839)

body at his first breath through the lungs, insert himself in the blood stream and makes his home in the heart (right atrium and right ventricle) of the baby.

Prophet Muhammad^{SAW} has also stated that demon (devil Jinn) is circulating with blood.[c] The companion demon having made his home in the heart, probably roams around in the human body through arteries and veins. He has thus access to almost any part of the human body. Other demons come and go, but the companion demon stays in the human body.

Since carbon dioxide is the food for demons, the companion demon probably consumes a part of the carbon dioxide formed in the human body as a result of the breakdown of carbohydrate. He must leave at the time of death, since the body stops making carbon dioxide. Because of his longevity, he probably occupies another human body.

The Activities of the Demons:
The demons are the foot soldiers of Satan. They are busy

---

[c] Satan runs in the body of Adam's son (i.e. man) as his blood circulates in it, and I was afraid that he (Satan) might insert an evil thought in your hearts. (Bukhari: 8.238, 3.255)

Satan reaches everywhere in the human body as blood reaches in it, (everywhere in one's body). I was afraid lest Satan might insert an evil thought in your minds. (Bukhari: 3.251)

Satan circulates in the human being as blood circulates in the body, and I was afraid lest Satan might insert an evil thought in your minds. (Bukhari: 3.254, 4.501)

Verily Satan circulates in the body like blood. (Muslim: 5404)

Satan penetrates in man like the penetration of blood (in every part of body). (Muslim: 5405)

Verily Satan flows in the blood stream of Adam's descendent. (Sunan Abu Dawood)[9]

Verily Satan influences arteries and veins through blood. (Bukhari and Muslim)[10]

implementing the orders of Satan. He sends them all over the world to carry out his orders.[d]

Being the foot soldiers of Satan they are involved in the same activities employed by Satan, which have been discussed in detail in Chapter 15 (The Power and Influence of Satan). They employ the tricks used by Satan. We will briefly describe these tricks here.

(a) They inspire greed of wealth [2:268]. Any moral action whether standing up for justice or helping others has its worldly consequences. The person may fear the loss of his job or his hard-earned money. It is the greed of wealth, inspired by the demons, that keeps the person from converting his conviction into action.

(b) They put fear in their heart of Satan's friends [3:175]. The friends of Satan seem to have power, glory, and an abundance of wealth in this life, at least in the short term. Standing up against them may throw shiver in the hearts of well-intentioned people. The demons are responsible for inculcating this fear.

(c) They sow the seed of dissension between husband and wife, brothers and sisters, friends, relatives, communities, and nations [5:91, 12:5, 17:53]. This brings conflict, war, and misery to both the parties. One of the tool they use to sow dissension is the promotion of gambling, alcohol, and drugs.

(d) They paint a beautiful picture of shameful and wrong things [2:268, 6:43, 8:48, 15:39-40, 16:63, 24:21, 27:24]. Even intelligent and skillful people can fall into this trap [29:38]. Any

---

[d] The throne of Iblis is upon the ocean and he sends detachments (to different parts) in order to put people to trial and the most important figure in his eyes is one who is most notorious in sowing the seed of dissension. (Muslim: 6754)

Iblis places his throne upon water. He then sends detachments (for creating dissension). The nearer to him in rank are those who are most notorious in creating dissension. One of them comes and says: I did so and so. And he says: You have done nothing. Then one amongst them comes and says: I did not spare so and so until I sowed the seed of discord between a husband and wife. The Satan goes near him and says: You have done well. He then embraces him. (Muslim: 6755)

shameful act is deplorable in its true form, but the demons do a good job of packaging it in such a manner that it looks beautiful. Promotion of nudity and vulgarity in the media is an excellent example of packaging shameful acts in alluring form. Nobody likes bad things done to him or her, but they do not mind doing the same to others.

(e) They give false hopes and create false desires [4:120, 17:64, 47:25]. The story of Yousuf^{AS} and his brothers is a good example of how Satan created false desires among his brothers. They thought that by getting rid of Yousuf^{AS}, they would get more love from Yaqoob^{AS} [12:8-9].

(f) They make us forget the good things [6:68, 12:42, 18:63, 20:115, 58:19]. If they cannot make us forget the good thing, they distract us from doing good [Bukhari 4.504, 511].

(g) They inspire secret counsel to promote iniquity and hostility and disobedience to the authorities [58:9-10]. Most of the conspiracies are hatched in secret, which can only bring chaos and anarchy in a society.

(h) They mislead by playing with our selfish desires and instincts [3:14, 11:15-16, 18:7, 28:15, 57:20, 102:1-2]. The self by nature is programmed to preserve its existence in this life. Every living organism does its best to protect itself from dangers, either by fighting the danger or by running away from it. This phenomenon is called 'fight or flight' in biology. In doing so it acts in a selfish manner, which is good to a certain extent. When this nature becomes so dominant that it transgresses all the limits, it becomes evil. The demons capitalize on this human nature.

(i) They can cause mental ailment (2:275). The Gospels mention four instances when Prophet Jesus (Isa^{AS}) cast out demons from men. In the first instance[e] he cast out devil who caused the person to become dumb. The person started speaking after the devil was cast out. In the second instance[f] he cast out an

---

[e] As they went out, behold, they brought to him a dumb man possessed with a devil (Luke calls dumb devil). And when the devil was cast out, the dumb spake. (Matthew 9:32-33, Luke 11:14)

[f] And there was in their synagogue a man with an unclean spirit; and he cried out, saying, Let us alone; what have we have to do with thee, thou

unclean spirit from a man in a synagogue. In the third instance[g] he cast out an unclean spirit (or devil) called legion from a person (or two) who used to dwell in tombs. In the fourth instance[h] he cast out the unclean spirit form a child.

Jesus of Nazareth? Art thou come to destroy us? I know thee who thou art, the Holy One of God. And Jesus rebuked him, saying, Hold thy peace, and come out of him. And when the unclean spirit had torn him, and cried with a loud voice, he came out of him. (Mark 1: 23-26, Luke 4:33-35)

[g] And they came over unto the other side of the sea, into the country of the Ger-ge-senes. And when he was come out of the ship, immediately there met him out of the tombs a man (two in Mathew) with an unclean spirit (devil in Mathew and Luke), who had his dwelling among the tombs; and no man could bind him, no, not with chains. Because that he had been often bound with fetters and chains, and the chains had been plucked asunder by him, and the fetters broken in pieces: neither could any man tame him. And always, night and day, he was in mountains, and in the tombs, crying, and cutting himself with stones. But when he saw Jesus afar off, he ran and worshipped him. And cried with a loud voice, and said, What have I to do with thee, Jesus, thou Son of the most high God? I adjure thee by God that thou torment me not. For he said unto him, Come out of the man, thou unclean spirit. And he asked him, What is thy name? And he answered, saying, My name is Legion: for we are many. And he besought him much that he would not send them out of the country. Now there was there nigh unto the mountains a great herd of swine feeding. And all the devils besought him, saying, Send us into the swine, that we may enter into them. And forthwith Jesus gave them leave. And the unclean spirits went out and entered into the swine: and herd ran violently down a steep place into the sea, (they were about two thousand;) and were choked in the sea. And they that fed the swine fled, and told it in the city, and in the country. And they went out to see what it was that was done. And they came to Jesus, and see him that was possessed with the devil, and had the legion, sitting, and clothed, and in his right mind: and they were afraid. (Mark 5:1-15, Matthew 8:28-33, Luke 8:26-36)

[h] And when he came to his disciples, he saw a great multitude about them, and the scribes questioning with them. And straightway all of the people, when they beheld him, were greatly amazed, and running to him saluted him. And he asked the scribes, What question ye with them. And one of the multitude answered and said, Master, I have

The brain activity is a very complex psychological phenomenon and requires a delicate electrical and chemical balance. We know that a sudden financial or emotional disaster or shock sometimes causes heart attack or mental instability. People who are familiar with the Holy Quran know that emotional and financial loses are test from God. Good humans remain calm when they suffer any calamity. People, who give up the remembrance of God, become materialistic and are mentally (psychologically) unprepared to handle calamities [10:11, 11:9-11, 41:49]. Since the demons have access to the brain, they may disturb the electrical and chemical balance in the brain of those who give up the remembrance of God, causing them to go crazy.

(j) They can also cause physical ailments. Their touch can also cause disease, as it happened with Prophet Job (Ayoob^{AS}) [21:83, 38:41]. He was covered with sores from head to toe, which he attributed to the touch of Satan. Since Satan and

---

brought unto thee my son, which has a dumb spirit (in Mathew he calls his son a lunatick and sore vexed); And wheresoever he taketh him, he teareth him; and he foameth, and gnasheth with his teeth, and pineth away: and I spake to thy disciples that they should cast him out; and they could not. He answereth him, and saith, O faithless generation, how long shall I suffer you? Bring him unto me. And they brought him unto him: and when he saw him, straightaway the spirit tare him; and he fell on the ground, and wallowed foaming. And he asked his father, How long ago since this came unto him? And he said, of a child. And oftimes it hath cast him into the fire, and into the waters, to destroy him: but if thou canst do any thing, have compassion on us, and help us. Jesus said unto him, If thou canst believe, all things are possible to him that believeth. And straightaway the father of the child cried out, and said with tears, Lord, I believe; help thou mine unbelief. When Jesus saw that the people came running together, he rebuked the foul spirit, saying unto him, Thou dumb and deaf spirit, I charge thee, come out of him, and enter no more into him (in Mathew Jesus rebuked the devil and in Luke he rebuked the unclean spirit). And the spirit cried, and rent him sore, and came out of him: and he was as one dead; in so much that many said, He is dead. But Jesus took him by the hand, and lifted him; and he arose. And when he was come into the house, his disciples asked him privately, Why could not we cast him out? And he said unto them, This kind can come forth by nothing, but prayer and fasting. (Mark 9:14-28, Matthew 17:14-21, Luke 9:37-43)

the demons can penetrate into the human body, they may be able to affect the chemical balance in the blood or the body to cause sores or other ailments. The distress in life is also a test in this life. It is a test of how patient we are and to whom do we turn to under distress. Those who do not put their trust in God seek refuge with the demons [4:38, 72:6]. The response of Prophet Job (Ayoob^{AS}) is a shining example of the power of patience. He patiently bore his distress, put his trust in God and only took refuge with him. Eventually he was cured.

The only power the demons have over humans is the power of suggestion, seduction, and persuasion.^{i} They are usually the instigators of bad thoughts in the human being. In such situations the Holy Quran advises us to seek refuge with God from Satan, the Cursed).^{j}

The Population of the Demons:
We made a case that every human being is accompanied by a demon. Since the human population is over six billion, there must be at least six billion companion demons. In addition there are demons that carry Satan's message to the companion demons. Assuming there could be one messenger demon for every six companion demons, there could be at least seven billion demons in the world.

---

^{i} O ye Children of Adam! Let not Satan seduce you --- (7:27)

(Iblees said:) "By Your power I will seduce all of them (human being) except Your purified servants." (38:82-83)

^{j} If a suggestion from Satan assails your (mind), seek refuge with God, for He hears and knows (all things). Those who fear God, when a thought of evil from Satan assaults them, bring God to remembrance, when lo! They see (aright). (7: 200-201)

Say: I seek refuge with the Lord and Cherisher of Mankind (*an-naas*), The King (or Ruler) of Mankind, The God (or Judge) of Mankind - From the mischief of the whisperer (of Evil), who withdraws (after his whisper) - (The same) who whispers into the hearts of Mankind (an-naas) - Among Jinns and among Men. (114: 1-6)

Summary:
The demons are the evil Jinns. There could be at least seven billion demons in the world. They possess all the characteristics and abilities the Jinns possess. They follow the orders of Satan who is bent on misguiding the humans. The only power the demons have over them is to plant evil ideas in their mind. They use this power to persuade and seduce. They feed bad ideas to our mind when we are awake as well as when we are asleep (in the form of bad dreams). They establish first contact when we are born and continue to attack us until the day we die. They use many tricks to achieve their objective. They inspire greed of wealth, fear of their votaries, sow seeds of dissension among people, paint beautiful picture of shameful and wrong things, give false hopes, create false desires, make us forget good things, inspire secret counsel to promote iniquity and hostility, and misleads us. They can also affect the human being by their touch, which can cause mental ailment. But this can only happen to people who have not mentally prepared themselves for the calamities they may face as a part of the test of this life. Their touch may also cause disease, which is also a test of this life.

Their power and tricks are not as strong as it seems. However, those who give up the remembrance of God, do not put their trust in Him, take Satan as their patron, join partners with God, and practice lying and cheating become their victims. The human being can protect him from the demons' attack and tricks by taking protection with God.

Chapter 27
The Angels, the Demons, Satan, the Jinns, and Humans

The life form we are familiar with is of cellular origin. This includes animals, plants, fungi, protista, and monera. The cell is their basic building block, which contains about 70 to 80 percent water and 20 to 30 percent solid substances such as organic compounds and minerals. The human being is the most complex and most intelligent being of this life form. Throughout the history, however, various kinds of beliefs have existed about spiritual beings. They have been categorized as good, bad or neutral beings with respect to how they affect the human being. They assume various forms in the religions of the world, which include celestial and atmospheric beings, devils, demons, and evil spirits; ghosts, ghouls, and goblins; and nature spirits and fairies[1]. In Western religions the good spiritual beings are usually called angels and the bad ones are termed demons. In Eastern, ancient, and primitive religions such beings are less categorical. For they may be good in some circumstances and bad in others[1]. Islam classifies spiritual beings into angels (*malaikah*) and the Jinns.[1]

Our investigation based on the Quranic statements and current scientific understanding suggests that the Jinns and the angels belong to two different worlds. The angels are energy beings and are made from photons. (According to another interpretation, the angels could be behind the three fundamental forces of nature: electromagnetic, nuclear, and gravitational forces.) The Jinns are gaseous beings and are probably made from carbon dioxide gas. The angels, being of photonic origin, possess no mass and travel at the speed of light (670 million miles per hour). The Jinns, being of gaseous origin, are probably 10 to 10,000 trillion times lighter than humans, and travel at the speed of sound (850 miles per hour). Due to their origin, both the angels and the Jinns are invisible and imperceptible and have the ability to penetrate human body. Since the angels are made from photons and the Jinns are made from gases, the angels have much more penetrative power than the Jinns. Again due to their photonic origin, the angels possess much more energy and power than the Jinns. The angels being made form photons are shaped in the form of wave. Their size will depend upon the frequency of the photon they are made from, but they do not occupy any space. The Jinns, being made from gas, have flexible size and shape, but should occupy space. They both also have the ability to transform into human form. The angels and the Jinns can both travel in space. However, whereas the reach of the angels is throughout the universe, the Jinns can only climb to an altitude of about 60 to 70 miles. Compared to the present human population of over six billion, the population of the angels is estimated to be at least 400 trillion, the population of the Jinns is estimated to be over ten billion, and the population of the demons is estimated to be over seven billion.

The angels could have been born about a million years after the creation of the universe. The Jinns were probably born soon after the creation of the earth. Compared to them, humans have only been in existence for less than one or two million years. The angels will not die until the end of the universe. Since the age of the universe is about 15 billion years, the age of each angel could be about the same. The Jinns, like humans, have a limited life span, but probably is ten times that of the humans. The angels do not procreate and have no gender. The Jinns, like humans, procreate and have gender. The angels probably consume photons to do work. The Jinns probably consume carbon dioxide gas to maintain their body and to do work. Since the angels do not die, their population should remain the same over the age of the universe. Since the Jinns are made from carbon dioxide gas, their population should depend upon the amount of carbon dioxide in the atmosphere. Our guess is that they were most populous about 1,900 million years ago. Since then their population probably started declining until the carbon dioxide gas concentration leveled off about few hundred million years ago. They were probably the most dominant species on the earth before the appearance of humans.

Both the angels and the Jinns, like humans, are intellectual beings. They possess knowledge, power of communication, and intelligence. The angels directly communicate with God. The Jinns can see and listen to the communication of the angels when they are within the flying range of the Jinns. Both the angels and the Jinns can listen to human conversation, but the humans cannot listen to their conversation. They also have the ability to communicate with humans without them knowing about it. The humans in general do not have such ability. The Prophets and the people of knowledge do have the ability to initiate conversation with the Jinns, but not with the angels. Both the angels and the Jinns are, however, inferior to the humans.

The angels do not have a free will and are busy executing the commands of God. The Jinns, like humans, have a free will, have been given guidance, created to worship God, and are expected to believe in the same things the human being is expected to believe in. Since the angels have no free will, there will be no reward or punishment for them on the day of Judgement. The Jinns, like humans, will be accountable for their deeds on the Day of Judgement and will either be enjoying the Paradise or suffering in the Hell. The angels will still be executing the commands of God. The characteristics of the angels, the Jinns, and the human are compared in Table 1.

Satan belongs to the class of the Jinns and possesses all the characteristics of the Jinns, except that he conversed with God at the time of the creation of Adam^{AS} and will live until the end of the world. He, like all the other Jinns, was created to worship God. He believed in the oneness of God, His Sovereignty, and His Lordship, and the Day of Judgment. But upon the creation of Adam^{AS}, he refused to bow to him and became a rebel. He is called the cursed one, the evil (*al-shaytan*), and the rejected (*al-rajeem*). God has given him reprieve until the end of the world. As such his age could be the age of the humanity, which means he could be at least about one or two million years old. He will be resurrected on the Day of Judgment, and will be accountable for his deeds. He will accept the falsehood of his actions and will go to the Hell. Satan is an enemy of the human being. Whereas the angels persuade humans to do good things, Satan and his agents persuade him to do evil things.

The demons are the bad Jinns. Every human has a permanent companion demon attached to him. Considering the current human population of over six billion, there could be at least seven billion demons in the world. They possess all the characteristics and abilities the Jinns possess. They are the foot soldiers of Satan and follow his orders. They are busy misguiding humans from the ways of God. However, the only power the demons have over them is to plant evil ideas in their mind. They use this power to persuade and seduce. They use many tricks to achieve his objective. They inspire greed of wealth, fear of their votaries, sow seeds of dissension among people, paint beautiful picture of shameful and wrong things, give false hopes, create false desires, make us forget good things, inspire secret counsel to promote iniquity and hostility, and mislead us. They can also affect the human being by their touch, which can cause mental ailment. Their touch may also cause disease, which is also a test of this life.

The power and tricks of Satan and the demons are not as strong as it seems. However, those who give up the remembrance of God, do not put their trust in Him, take Satan as their patron, join partners with God, and practice lying and cheating become their victims. The human being can protect him from the demons' attack and tricks by taking protection with God.

Table I
A Comparison among the Angels, the Jinns, and the Humans

	The Angels	The Jinns	Humans
Basic Building Block Type	Photons	Carbon dioxide molecules	Organic cell
Mass of the Basic Building Block	Zero	7.3×10^{-23} gm	6×10^{-7} to 6×10^{-10} gm
Size of the Basic Building Block	3×10^{-9} to 3×10^{14} micron	0.002 micron	10 to 100 micron
State	Electromagnetic Wave (light)	Gas	Solid
Shape	Wave	Flexible	Fixed
Size	Wavelength of photon	Flexible	Fixed
Volume	No	Yes	Yes
Speed	670 million miles per hour	850 miles per hour	4 to 15 miles per hour
Reach	The whole Universe	Altitude of 60 to 70 miles	Cannot fly on their own

Table I (continued)
A Comparison among the Angels, the Jinns, and the Humans

	The Angels	The Jinns	Humans
Time of Appearance	15 billion years ago	4.8 billion years ago	<2 million years ago
Life Span	Life of the Universe	About 500 to 1,000 years	About 60 to 100 years
Gender	No	Yes	Yes
Procreation	No	Yes	Yes
Food	Photons	Carbon dioxide	Fruit, vegetable, and animal meat
Free Will	No	Yes	Yes
Energy		25,000 ft-lbf/lb*	~10 ft-lbf/lb*

Calculated based on kinetic energy formula of $(1/2) \times mass \times velocity^2$. Used 850 miles per hour for the Jinns and 15 miles per hour for the humans.

APPENDICES

Appendix A
Satan and Adam^{AS}
The Sequence of the Quranic Events

Background:

We created man from sounding clay from mud molded into shape (15-26)

And the Jinn race We had created before from the fire of a scorching wind (15-27)

Announcement:

Behold thy Lord said to the angels: "I will create a vicegerent on the earth." (2-30)

"I am about to create man from sounding clay from mud molded into shape; (15-28, 38-71)

"When I have fashioned him (in due proportion) and breathed into him of My spirit fall ye down in obeisance unto him." (15-29, 38-72)

They said "Wilt thou place therein one who will make mischief therein and shed blood? Whilst we do celebrate Thy praises and glorify Thy holy (name)?" He said: "I know what ye know not." (2-30

Creation:

It is We who created you and gave you shape; (7-11)

Appointment of Vicegerent:
And He taught Adam the nature of all things; then He placed them before the angels and said: "Tell Me the nature of these if ye are right." (2-31)
They said: "Glory to Thee of knowledge we have none save that Thou hast taught us: in truth it is Thou who art perfect in knowledge and wisdom." (2-32)
He said: "O Adam! tell them their natures." When he had told

them God said: "Did I not tell you that I know the secrets of heaven and the earth and I know what ye reveal and what ye conceal?" (2-33)

Order:
Then We bade the angels bow down to Adam and they bowed down; not so Iblis. (2-34, 7-11, 15-30, 31, 17-61, 18-50, 20-116, 38-73,74)

He was one of the Jinns, and he broke the command of his Lord. (18-50)

He refused to be of those who bow down. He was haughty and became one of those who reject Faith. (2-34, 7-11, 15-30, 31, 17-61, 20-116, 38-73,74)

God Asked Iblees:

"O Iblis! what prevented thee from bowing down when I commanded thee to one whom I have created with My hands? Art thou haughty? Or art thou one of the high (and mighty) ones?" (7-12, 38-75)

"O Iblis! what is your reason for not being among those who prostrated themselves?" (15-32)

Iblees Replied:

"Shall I bow down to one whom Thou didst create from clay?" (17-61)

"I am not one to prostrate myself to man whom thou didst create from sounding clay from mud molded into shape." (15-33)

"I am better than he: thou didst create me from fire and him from clay." (7-12, 38-76)

God Cursed Iblees:

"Get thee down from this: it is not for thee to be arrogant here: get out for thou art of the meanest (of creatures)." (7-13)

"Get thee out from here: for thou art rejected accursed. And My Curse shall be on thee till the Day of Judgement." (15-34,35, 38-77, 78)

Iblees Asked for Respite:

"O my Lord! give me then respite till the Day the (dead) are raised." (7-14, 15-36, 38-79)

"Seest Thou? This is the one whom thou hast honored above me! If Thou wilt but respite me to the Day of Judgment I will surely bring his descendants under my sway all but a few!" (17-62)

God Gave Respite:

"Respite is granted thee till the Day of the Time Appointed." (7-15, 15-37,38, 38-80,81)

Iblees Challenged:

"Because Thou hast thrown me out of the way lo! I will lie in wait for them on Thy straight way. (7-16)

"Then will I assault them from before them and behind them from their right and their left: nor wilt Thou find in most of them gratitude (for Thy mercies). (7-17)

"O my Lord! Because Thou hast put me in the wrong I will make (wrong) fair-seeming to them on the earth. Then by Thy power I will put them all in the wrong, except Thy Servants amongst them sincere and purified (by Thy grace)." (15-39, 40, 38-82, 83)

"I will take of Thy servants a portion marked off. I will mislead them and I will create in them false desires; I will order them to slit the ears of cattle and to deface the (fair) nature created by God." (4-118, 119) Whoever forsaking God takes Satan for a friend hath of a surety suffered a loss that is manifest. (4-119)

God's Response to the Challenge:

"Then it is just and fitting and I say what is just and fitting" (38-84)

"Get out from this disgraced and expelled. I will certainly fill Hell with thee and those that follow thee--every one. (7-18, 17-63, 38-85)

"Lead to destruction those whom thou canst among them with thy (seductive) voice; make assaults on them with thy cavalry and thy infantry; mutually share with them wealth and children;

and make promises to them. But Satan promises them nothing but deceit. (17-64)

"This (Way of My sincere servants) is indeed a Way that leads straight to Me. (15-41)

"For over My servants no authority shalt thou have except such as put themselves in the wrong and follow thee." (15-42, 17-65)

And verily Hell is the promised abode for them all! (15-43)

To it are seven Gates: for each of those Gates is (special) class (of sinners assigned). (15-44)

Satan's First Victim:

We said: "O Adam! dwell thou and thy wife in the garden and eat of the bountiful things therein as (where and when) ye will but approach not this tree or ye run into harm and transgression." (2-35, 7-19)

Then We said: "O Adam! verily this is an enemy to thee and thy wife: so let him not get you both out of the Garden so that thou art landed in misery. There is therein (enough provision) for thee not to go hungry nor to go naked. Nor to suffer from thirst nor from the sun's heat " (20-117, 118, 119)

Then began satan to whisper suggestions to them bringing openly before their minds all their shame that was hidden from them (before). (7-20)

He said " O Adam! shall I lead thee to Tree of Eternity and to a kingdom that never decays?" (20-120) "Your Lord only forbade you this tree lest ye should become angels or such beings as live for ever." (7-20) And he swore to them both that he was their sincere adviser. (7-21)

Then did Satan make them slip from the (garden) and get them out of the state (of felicity) in which they had been. (2-36)

By deceit he brought about their fall: when they tasted of the tree their shame became manifest to them and they began to sew together the leaves of the garden over their bodies. (7-22, 20-121)

Thus did Adam disobey His Lord and allow himself to be seduced. (20-121)

And their Lord called unto them: "Did I not forbid you that tree and tell you that Satan was an avowed enemy unto you?" (7-22)

They said: "our Lord! we have wronged our own souls: if Thou forgive us not and bestow not upon us Thy mercy we shall certainly be lost." (7-23)

(God) said: "Get ye down with enmity between yourselves. On the earth will be your dwelling-place and your means of livelihood for a time." (7-24, 2-36) "Therein shall ye live and therein shall ye die; but from it shall ye be taken out (at last)." (7-25)

Then learnt Adam from his Lord words of inspiration and his Lord turned toward him; for He is Oft-Returning Most Merciful. (2-37)

But his Lord chose him (for His Grace): He turned to him and gave him guidance. (20-122)

He said: "Get ye down both of you all together from the Garden with enmity one to another; but if as is sure there comes to you guidance from Me whosoever follows My guidance will not lose his way nor fall into misery. (20-123) "On them shall be no fear nor shall they grieve. (2-38)

"But whosoever turns away from My Message verily for him is a life narrowed down and We shall raise him up blind on the Day of Judgment." (20-124) "They shall be Companions of the Fire; they shall abide therein." (2-39)

Appendix B
Electromagnetic Waves

A wave is a periodic disturbance (certain changes that repeat themselves again and again in time) that transports energy from one place to another.[1] A wave is characterized by three terms: wavelength, frequency, and amplitude. 'The wavelength is the distance between successive peaks or successive troughs of the waves. The frequency refers to the number of up-and-down cycles of oscillation that a wave completes every second. The term amplitude refers to the maximum height or depth of a wave.'[2] Most waves, like sound waves and water waves, require material medium to transfer energy. For example, sound waves require the molecules of air and water waves require the molecules of water. The electromagnetic waves do not require any medium for their propagation. All electromagnetic waves are of the same basic nature and travel at the same speed in vacuum. They differ only in their frequency and wavelength.[3] The following is a brief description of these waves[4]:

> **Radio Waves:** Radio waves are produced by accelerating charges though conducting wires. Their wavelength is 1 meter or more. They are used in radio and television communication system.
>
> **Microwaves:** Microwaves (short-wavelength radio waves) are generated by electronic device. They have wavelength ranging between about 1 millimeter and 30 centimeter. They are used in microwave oven, radar system for aircraft navigation and for studying atomic and molecular properties of matter.
>
> **Infrared waves:** Infrared waves are sometimes called heat waves. These waves are produced by hot bodies and molecules and have wavelengths ranging from about 1 millimeter to 7×10^{-7} meter. These waves are readily

absorbed by most materials resulting in heating of the material. These waves are used in physical therapy, infrared photography, and the study of the vibrations of atoms.

Visible light: Visible light is the most common form of electromagnetic waves. It is that part of electromagnetic waves that is detected by the human eye. It is produced by the rearrangement of electrons in atoms and molecules. The wavelength of visible light ranges from 4×10^{-7} meter (violet color) to 7×10^{-7} meter (red color).

Ultraviolet (UV) Ray: The ultraviolet rays are produced by the sun. Their wavelength ranges from about 4×10^{-7} meter (400 nanometer) down to 6×10^{-10} meter (0.6 nanometer). Most of the ultraviolet waves from the sun is absorbed by atoms in the upper atmosphere (stratosphere), which warms the stratosphere.

X-rays: X-rays are produced by bombarding metals with accelerated high-energy electrons. Their wavelength ranges from about 10^{-8} meter (10 nanometer) to 10^{-13} meter (10^{-4} nanometer). They are used as a diagnostic tool in medicine and as a treatment for certain form of cancer.

Gamma Rays: Gamma rays are emitted by radioactive nuclei. Their wavelength ranges from about 10^{-10} meter to less than 10^{-14} meter. They are highly penetrating and cause serious damage when absorbed by living tissues.

Cosmic Rays: Cosmic rays are highly energetic (few billion to ten million billion electron volts) very fast moving particles bombarding the earth from outer space.[5]

The wavelength, the frequency, and the energy of these electromagnetic waves are shown in Table 1. Each type of wave has a peculiar wavelength range and energy. The energy of these waves ranges from 4×10^{17} electron volts to 4×10^{-13} electron volts. The shorter the wavelength higher is the energy of the wave.

Table 1
The Characteristics of the Electromagnetic Waves[1]

Electromagnetic Waves	Wavelength (m)	Frequency (sec^{-1})	Photon Energy (eV)	Typical Source
Cosmic ray	3×10^{-15}	10^{23}	4×10^8	Astronomical
Gamma rays	3×10^{-14}	10^{22}	4×10^7	Radioactive nuclei
Gamma rays, X-rays	3×10^{-13}	10^{21}	4×10^6	
X-rays	3×10^{-12}	10^{20}	4×10^5	Electron impact on a solid
Soft x-rays	3×10^{-11}	10^{19}	4×10^4	Atomic inner shell
Ultraviolet, X-rays	3×10^{-10}	10^{18}	4×10^3	Atoms in sparks
Ultraviolet	3×10^{-9}	10^{17}	4×10^2	Atoms in sparks and arcs
Ultraviolet	3×10^{-8}	10^{16}	4×10^1	Atoms in sparks and arcs
Visible light	3×10^{-7}	10^{15}	4	Atoms, hot bodies, molecules

Table 1 (continued)
The Characteristics of the Electromagnetic Waves[1]

Electromagnetic Waves	Wavelength (m)	Frequency (sec^{-1})	Photon Energy (eV)	Typical Source
Infrared	3×10^{-6}	10^{14}	4×10^{-1}	Hot bodies, molecules
Infrared	3×10^{-5}	10^{13}	4×10^{-2}	Hot bodies, molecules
Far-infrared	3×10^{-4}	10^{12}	4×10^{-3}	Hot bodies, molecules
Microwaves	3×10^{-3}	10^{11}	4×10^{-4}	Electronic devices
Microwaves, Radar	3×10^{-2}	10^{10}	4×10^{-5}	Electronic devices
Radar, Interstellar Hydrogen	3×10^{-1}	10^{9}	4×10^{-6}	Electronic devices
Television, FM Radio	3	10^{8}	4×10^{-7}	Electronic devices
Short-wave Radio	3×10^{1}	10^{7}	4×10^{-8}	Electronic devices
AM Radio	3×10^{2}	10^{6}	4×10^{-9}	Electronic devices

Table 1 (continued)
The Characteristics of the Electromagnetic Waves[1]

Electro magnetic Waves	Wave- length (m)	Fre- quency (sec^{-1})	Photon Energy (eV)	Typical Source
Long-wave Radio	3×10^3	10^5	4×10^{-10}	Electronic devices
Induction Heating	3×10^4	10^4	4×10^{-11}	Electronic devices
	3×10^5	10^3	4×10^{-12}	Electronic devices
Power	3×10^6	10^2	4×10^{-13}	Rotating machinery
Power	3×10^7	10	4×10^{-14}	Rotating machinery
	3×10^8	1	4×10^{-15}	Commutated direct current
Direct Current	Infinity	0	4×10^{-16}	Batteries

[1] McGraw-Hill Encyclopedia of Science and Technology, 6th Edition, McGraw-Hill Book Company, New York, 1987, p.155.

Appendix C
The Origin of the Angels
– the Other Possibility

Scientists have identified three force particles that have no mass: photons, gluons, and gravitons.[1] These particles are associated with three fundamental forces: electromagnetic force, the strong force, and gravitational force.[2] Another force particle, called weak gauge bosons, come in varieties with 86 and 97 times the mass of proton and is associated with the weak force.[3]

Gravity was the closest to our everyday experience before the advent of electronics and still is to a greater extent. It keeps us firmly planted on the earth and keeps the moon in orbit around the earth and the earth in orbit around the sun. It is responsible for forming most structures in the universe, including galaxies, stars, and planets.

The electromagnetic force is responsible for keeping electrons in orbit around the nucleus. It is ultimately responsible for the existence of atoms and molecules, and hence is the basis of life. It holds our bones and skins together. Although the electromagnetic force is intrinsically much stronger than gravity, its influence is limited within atoms.[4] In modern life, the electromagnetic force is also responsible for driving lights, computers, radio, telephones, television, many kitchen appliances, and many other conveniences.

Whereas gravity is responsible for holding solar system together and electromagnetic force is responsible for keeping atom together, the strong nuclear force is responsible for holding the nucleus of the atoms together. The strong forces keeps the elementary particles (quarks) glued inside protons and neutrons and keep protons and neutrons tightly crammed together inside atomic nuclei. Although it is intrinsically the strongest of the four forces, the strong force has very short range of influence. The range of the strong nuclear force is about the size of a large atomic nucleus, about ten thousand times smaller than the size of an atom (about 10^{-12} centimeters). The strong force drives the process of nuclear fusion, which in turn provides most of the energy in stars and hence in the universe at the present epoch. The large magnitude of the strong force in comparison with the electromagnetic force is ultimately the reason why nuclear reactions are much more powerful (by a factor of a million on a particle-by particle basis[5]) than chemical reactions.

The strong force is the strongest and the gravitational force is the weakest of all the forces. The characteristics of these particles are shown in Table 1. Except for gravitons, the existence of the other force particles has been experimentally confirmed.[6]

The weak nuclear force 'mediates the decay of neutrons into protons, and also plays a role in nuclear fusion, radioactivity, and the production of the elements in the stars. The weak force has an even shorter range than the strong force. In spite of its weak strength and short range, the weak force plays a surprisingly important role in astrophysics. A substantial fraction of the total mass of the universe is most likely made up of weakly interacting particles, in other words, particles that interact only through the weak force and gravity. Because such particles tend to interact on very long time scales, they play an increasingly important role as the universe slowly cranks through its future history.'[7]

Since, by definition, the angels are made from mass-less particles traveling at the speed of light; they could have been made from photons, gravitons, and gluons. Since bosons possess mass, they cannot be the basic constituents of the angels.

Type of Angels:

The Holy Quran also tells us that there are three types of angels.[a] Though the angels are made from particles that move at the speed of light and thus have no mass, their strength varies: some have two wings, some have three wings, and some have four

---

[a] Praise be to God Who created (out of nothing) the heavens and the earth Who made the angels messengers with wings two or three or four (Pairs): He adds to Creation as He pleases: for God has power over all things. (35:1)

wings. Scholars have taken wings to mean power or quality.[8,9] It could also imply influence. Accepting the proposition that the angels are made from photons, gravitons, and gluons, would imply that the angels will be of three types: some are made from photons, some from gravitons, and some from gluons. The strength or influence of the angels will depend upon the strength and influence of these particles. The strength of the angels made from gluons will be the strongest, but their influence will be limited. The strength of the angels made from photons will be stronger than those made from gravitons, but less than those made from gluons. However, their influence will be more than those made from gluons. The strength of the angels made from gravitons will be the weakest, but their influence will be more than those made from gluons.

Functions of the Angels:
According to the Holy Quran, the main function of the angels is to execute the command of God and convey his message.[b]

As mentioned earlier, photons, gravitons, gluons, and gauge bosons are the smallest constituents of electromagnetic, gravitational, strong and weak forces, respectively. These particles can also be thought of as microscopic transmitters of

---

[b] And by those who glide along (on errands of mercy). Then press forward as in a race. Then arrange to do (the commands of their Lord) (79:3-5)

O you who believe! Save yourselves and your families from a Fire whose fuel is Men and Stones over which are (appointed) angels stern (and) severe who flinch not (from executing) the Commands they receive from God but do (precisely) what they are commanded. (66:6)

We have indeed revealed this (Message) in the night of Power: And what will explain to you what the Night of Power is? The Night of Power is better than a thousand Months. Therein come down the angels and the Spirit by God's permission on every errand: Peace!... This until the rise of Morn! (97:1-5)

Praise be to God Who created (out of nothing) the heavens and the earth Who made the angels messengers with wings two or three or four (Pairs): He adds to Creation as He pleases: for God has power over all things. (35:1)

the respective forces. That is why these force particles are also called the messenger particles of the respective forces. [10] Photons, gravitons, gluons, and bosons transmit the electromagnetic, gravitational, strong and weak forces, respectively. According to Greene, the photon is the transmitter of a message of how the recipient must respond to the electromagnetic force. If the two particles are of same charge, the photon carries the message "move apart." On the other hand if the two particles are of opposite charge, the photon carries the message "come together." [11]

Just as photons are the electromagnetic force's messenger particles, gravitons are the gravitational force's messenger particles. When you drop a glass, 'you can think of the event in terms of the earth's gravitational field pulling on the glass' or 'you can also think of it in terms of graviton particles firing back and forth between the earth and the glass, communicating a gravitational "message" that "tells" the glass to fall toward the earth.'[12] Similarly the strong force 'arises from individual quarks exchanging gluons' and the weak force 'is mediated by the weak gauge bosons.'[13]

Food:
Accepting this explanation would imply that the angels made from gluons, photons, and gravitons will consume gluons, photons, and graviton, respectively, to do purposeful work (see Chapter 19).

Purposeful Work:
Accepting the proposition that the angels are made from photons, gravitons, and gluons would imply that they draw energy by consuming these particles (packets of energy) to do the work. This will be no different from the fact that humans and other animals made from cells, draw energy by consuming food of cellular origin.

It is a common observation that most of the activity around the earth is based on the solar energy. It is the solar energy that puts the wind in motion and evaporates water from the ocean to form cloud. As the rainwater flows through river, it moves boats, breaks rocks into sand, irrigates fields, produces electricity, and etc. The wind also drives the ships in ocean. It is the water and solar energy (and carbon dioxide) which produces vegetation, which is the source of food for animals. It is the wood (a form of dried vegetation) that used to be the source of energy in the past and still is in remote areas. It is also the vegetation buried under the earth for millions of years that is now used as coal, gas and oil. Most of the modern day communication is conducted through electromagnetic force. Electricity, which drives most of the communication equipment (radio, television, telephone, cellular phone and others) and the appliances is produced by hydropower, coal, or oil. Thus the source of most of the activity on the earth is the solar energy, which is basically a collection of photons.

    The photons in the sun and all the stars are generated by the nuclear reaction, which converts hydrogen into helium. It is the nuclear force or graviton that brings hydrogen atoms together to form helium that results in the creation of photons. In other words the nuclear force creates photons, which is carried by the electromagnetic force to the earth. And had it not been the gravitational force that is keeping all the planets in the solar system in their orbits, the whole system would have collapsed. We will, therefore, propose that the angels are behind the nuclear, electromagnetic force, and gravitational forces. This explains how the angels could be behind all the forces of nature that governs not just the earth but the whole universe.

Table 1
The Forces of Nature[1]

Force	Force Particle	Mass of the Force Particle *	Relative Strength of the Force Particles	Range of Influence of the Force
Strong	Gluon	0	10^{44}	Within the nucleus of an atom
Electromagnetic	Photon	0	10^{42}	Within the atom
Weak	Weak gauge bosons	86, 97	10^{39}	Within the neutron
Gravity	Graviton	0	1	Within the universe

* the rest mass (i.e. when the particle is at rest) in multiples of the proton mass.

[1] Greene, B., "The Elegant Universe," Vintage Books, New York, 2003, p. 11.

References

Chapter 1: Introduction
1. The New Encyclopedia Britannica, Encyclopedia Britannica, Inc., 1977, Volume 1, pp. 871-876.
2. Mawdudi, S.A.A., "Towards Understanding Islam," The Message Publications, New York, 1988, p.93.
3. Wiggin, K. D. and Smith, N. A. (ed.), "The Arabian Nights," Barnes and Noble Books, New York, 1993, pp. 52-57.
4. Al-Ashqar, U. S., "The World of the Jinn and Devils," Translated by Zarabozo, J. A. M., Al-Basheer Company for Publications and Translations, Boulder, Colorado, 1998.
5. Ashour, M., "The Jinn in the Quran and the Sunna," Translated by Bewley, A., Dar Al-Taqwa, London, 1993.
6. Philips, A. A. B., "Ibn Taymeeyah's Essay on the Jinn (Demons)," Tawheed Publications, Riyadh, Saudi Arabia, 1989.
7. Sakr, A. H., "Al-Jinn," Foundation for Islamic Knowledge, Lombard, Illinois, 1994.

Chapter 2: The Origin of the Jinns
1. The Holy Quran: Surah Al-Anaam, Verses 100, 112, 128, and 130; Surah Al-Aaraaf, Verses 38 and 179; Surah Al-Isra, Verse 88; Surah Al-Kahf, Verse 50; Surah An-Naml, Verses 17 and 39; Surah Saba, Verses 12, 14, and 41; Surah Fussilat, Verses 25 and 29; Surah Al-Ahqaaf, Verse 18 and 29; Surah Adh-Dhariyaata, Verse 56; Surah Ar-Rahmaan, Verse 33; and Surah Al-Jinn, Verses 1, 5, and 6.
2. The Holy Quran: Surah Al-Hijr, Verse 27; Surah Ar-Rahmaan, Verses 15, 39, 56, and 84.
3. The Holy Quran: Surah Hood, Verse 119; Surah As-Sijdah, Verse 13; Surah As-Saaffaat Verse 158; Surah An-Naas, Verse 6.
4. Abdullah Yusuf Ali, "The Meaning of the Holy Quran," Amana Publications, Beltsville, Maryland, 1989, Note No. 929 of Surah Al Anam, Verse 100.
5. Growing up with Science, H. S. Stuttman Inc., Westport, Connecticut, 1990, Volume 6, p. 528.
6. Lewis, B., and von Elbe, G., "Combustion, Flame, and Explosion of Gases," Academic Press, 1961, Chapter IX.
7. Welty, J. R., Wicks, C. E., and Wilson, R. E., "Fundamentals of Momentum, Heat and Mass Transfer," John Wiley and Sons, Inc., New

York, 1969, p.648.
8. CRC Handbook of Chemistry and Physics, CRC Press, Cleveland, Ohio, 56th Edition, 1975, p. B-84 and B-86.
9. Al-Hilali, M. T. and Khan, M. M., "The Noble Quran," Maktaba Dar-us-Salam, Riyadh, Saudi Arabia, 1993, Surah Ar-Raman, Verse 31.
10. Daryabadi, A. M., "Tafsir-ul-Quran," Darul-Ishaat, Karachi, Pakistan, 1991, Surah Ar-Raman, Verse 31.
11. Ali, A. Y., "The Meaning of the Holy Quran," Amana Publications, Beltsville, Maryland, 1989, Note No. 5193 of Surah Ar Rahman, Verse 31.
12. Miller, K. R. and Levine, J., "Biology," Prentice Hall, Englewood Cliffs, New Jersey, First Edition, 1991, pp. 159-165.
13. Slesnick, I. L., Balzer, L., McCormack, A. J., Newton, D. E., Rasmussen, F. A., "Scott, Foresman Biology," Scott, Foresman and Company, Glenview, Illinois, 1985, p. 99.
14. Sahih Muslim, Book of Al-Salaat, Chapter CLXXX, No. 903. (Volume 1, p.244 in English Translation by A. H. Siddiqui).

Chapter 3: The Physical Characteristics of the Jinns
1. Ganic, E. N. and Hicks, T.G.(ed.), "The McGraw-Hill Handbook of Essential Engineering Information and Data," McGraw-Hill, Inc., 1991, p. 4.1.
2. Welty, J.R., Wicks, C.E., Wilson, R.E., "Fundamentals of Momentum, Heat, and Mass Transfer," John Wiley & Sons, Inc., 1969, pp. 651-653.
3. CRC Handbook of Chemistry and Physics, CRC Press, Cleveland, Ohio, 56th Edition, 1975-1976, F-206.
4. The Random House Children's Encyclopedia, Random House, New York, 1991, p. 48.
5. The Random House Children's Encyclopedia, Random House, New York, 1991, pp. 21-22.
6. The New Encyclopedia Britannica, Encyclopedia Britannica, Inc., Volume 12, p. 36, 1977.
7. Sahih Muslim, (English Translation Only) Volume 3, p. 1188, Dar al Arabia, Beirut, Lebanon; Chapter CMIX, No. 5404.
8. Sahih Muslim, (English Translation Only) Volume 3, p. 1188, Dar al Arabia, Beirut, Lebanon; Chapter CMIX, No. 5405.
9. Sunan Abu Dawood, Volume 3, p. 1390, #4976.
10. Mufti Muhammad Shafi, "Maarif-ul-Quran," Adarah Al-Maarif, Karachi, Pakistan, 1988, Volume 8, page 853, Explanation of Surah An-Naas. Reported by Anas[RA] in Sahih Bukhari and Sahih Muslim.

11. Smith, J. M. and Van Ness, H. C., "Introduction to Chemical Engineering Thermodynamics," McGraw-Hill Book Co., 1959, p. 64.
12. Smith, J. M. and Van Ness, H. C., "Introduction to Chemical Engineering Thermodynamics," McGraw-Hill Book Co., 1959, Chap. 9.
13. Mufti Muhammad Shafi, "Maarif-ul-Quran," Adarah Al-Maarif, Karachi, Pakistan, 1988, Volume 4, page 256-258, Explanation of Ayah 48 of Surah Al-Anfal, reported by Ibn Jareer through Hadhrat Abdullah ibn Abbas[RA]
14. Tafseer Ibn Katheer, explanation of Ayah 48 of Surah Al-Anfal, reported by Tibrani through Rifaah bin Rafay[RA], by Urwah bin Zubair[RA], and by Abdullah ibn Abbas[RA].

Chapter 4: The Biological Characteristics of the Jinns
1. Lehninger, A.L., "Biochemistry," Worth Publishers, Inc., New York, 1975, p. 3.
2. Sahih Bukhari, LVIII, The Merits of Ansar, Chapter 31, No. 200.
3. Sunan Abu Dawood, Purification, Chapter 20, No. 39.
4. Sahih Muslim, Book of Al-Salaat, Chapter CLXXX, No. 903. (Volume 1, p.244 in English Translation by A. H. Siddiqui).
5. Abu Al Hasan, "The Jinn," Al-Jumuah Magazine Vol 8, Issue 3, Rabi Al-Awwal 1417 H, Islamic Revival Association, Madison, Wisconsin. Related by Al-Hakim
6. Lehninger, A. L., "Biochemistry," Worth Publishers, Inc., New York, 1975, pp.1031-1033.
7. The New Encyclopedia Britannica, Encyclopedia Britannica, Inc., 1977, Volume 2, pp. 313-317.
8. The Random House Children's Encyclopedia, Random House, New York, 1991, p. 174.
9. Mufti Muhammad Shafi, "Maarif-ul-Quran," Adarah Al-Maarif, Karachi, Pakistan, 1988, Volume 8, page 852-3," Explanation of Surah An-Naas. Reported Abu Yaali through Anas[RA] in Tafseer Mazhari.

Chapter 5: The Intellectual Ability of the Jinns
1. Hooper, J. and Teresi, D., "The Three-Pound Universe," G. P. Putnam's Sons, New York, 1986, pp. 53-59.
2. Mufti Muhammad Shafi, "Maarif-ul-Quran," Adarah Al-Maarif, Karachi, Pakistan, 1988, Volume 4, page 256-258, Explanation of Ayah 48 of Surah Al-Anfal, reported by Ibn Jareer through Hadhrat Abdullah ibn Abbas[RA]
3. Tafseer Ibn Katheer, explanation of Ayah 48 of Surah Al-Anfal, reported by Tibrani through Rifaah bin Rafay[RA], by Urwah bin Zubair[RA], and by Abdullah ibn Abbas[RA].

4. Mufti Muhammad Shafi, "Maarif-ul-Quran," Adarah Al-Maarif, Karachi, Pakistan, 1988, Volume 8, page 852-3," Explanation of Surah An-Naas. Reported Abu Yaali through Anas[RA] in Tafseer Mazhari.
5. Riyadh-us-Saleheen, Volume II, Chapter 303, No. 1668, p. 809, International Islamic Publishers, Karachi, Pakistan. 1986.

Chapter 6: The Spiritual Nature of the Jinns
No reference cited.

Chapter 7: The Difference Between the Jinns and the Humans
1. Abu Al Hasan, "The Jinn," Al-Jumuah Magazine Vol 8, Issue 3, Rabi Al-Awwal 1417 H, Islamic Revival Association, Madison, Wisconsin. Related by Al-Hakim
2. Lehninger, A. L., "Biochemistry," Worth Publishers, Inc., New York, 1975, pp.1031-1033.
3. The New Encyclopedia Britannica, Encyclopedia Britannica, Inc., 1977, Volume 2, pp. 313-317.
4. The Random House Children's Encyclopedia, Random House, New York, 1991, p. 174.
5. Saheeh Muslim, (English Translation Only) Volume 3, p.1188, Dar al Arabia, Beirut, Lebanon; Chapter CMIX, No. 5404,
6. Saheeh Muslim, (English Translation Only) Volume 3, p.1188, Dar al Arabia, Beirut, Lebanon; Chapter CMIX, No. 5405,
7. Sunan Abu Dawood, Volume 3, p.1390, #4976.
8. Mufti Muhammad Shafi, "Maarif-ul-Quran," Adarah Al-Maarif, Karachi, Pakistan, 1988, Volume 8, page 853, Explanation of Surah An-Naas. Reported by Anas[RA] in Saheeh Bukhari and Saheeh Muslim
9. Mufti Muhammad Shafi, "Maarif-ul-Quran," Adarah Al-Maarif, Karachi, Pakistan, 1988, Volume 8, page 852," Explanation of Surah An-Naas. Reported Abu Yaali through Anas[RA] in Tafseer Mazhari.
10. Riyadh-us-Saleheen, Volume II, Chapter 303, No. 1668, p. 809, International Islamic Publishers, Karachi, Pakistan. 1986.
11. The Random House Children's Encyclopedia, Random House, New York, 1991, pp. 265-266.
12. The Random House Children's Encyclopedia, Random House, New York, 1991, pp. 539-540.
13. The Random House Children's Encyclopedia, Random House, New York, 1991, pp. 95-96.
14. The Random House Children's Encyclopedia, Random House, New York, 1991, pp. 21-22.
15. The Random House Children's Encyclopedia, Random House, New York, 1991, pp. 641-642.

16. The Random House Children's Encyclopedia, Random House, New York, 1991, pp. 503-504.
17. The Random House Children's Encyclopedia, Random House, New York, 1991, p. 454.
18. The Random House Children's Encyclopedia, Random House, New York, 1991, p. 314.
19. Al-Hilali, M.T., and Khan, M. H., "The Noble Quran," Maktaba Dar-us-Salam, Riyadh, Saudi Arabia.
20. Growing up with Science, H. S. Stuttman Inc., Westport, Connecticut, 1990, Volume 16, p. 1428.
21. Dean, J. A. (ed.), "Lang's Handbook of Chemistry," 13th Ed., McGraw Hill, New York, 1985, page 3-2.
22. Growing up with Science, H. S. Stuttman Inc., Westport, Connecticut, 1990, Volume 14, pp 1276-1279.
23. Smith, J. M. and Van Ness, H. C., "Introduction to Chemical Engineering Thermodynamics," McGraw-Hill Book Co., 1959, Chap. 9.
24. Encylopaedia Britannica, 1977, Volume 3, p. 1045.
25. CRC Handbook of Chemistry and Physics, CRC Press, Cleveland, Ohio, 56th Edition, 1975, p. F-212 and F-214.
26. Miller, K. R. and Levine, J., "Biology," Prentice Hall, New Jersey, 1991, p. 86.
27. The Random House Children's Encyclopedia, Random House, New York, 1991, p. 490.

Chapter 8: Deriving Benefits from the Jinns
No reference cited.

Chapter 9: Myths about the Jinns
1. Shahab, Qudratullah, "Shahab Namah," San Mayl Publications, Lahore, Pakistan, 1999, pp. 246-257.

Chapter 10: Genie in the Bottle – An Analysis
1. Wiggin, K. D. and Smith, N. A. (ed.), "The Arabian Nights," Barnes and Nobles Books, New York, 1933, pp. 52-57.

Chapter 11: Summary
No reference cited.

Chapter 12: Who is Satan?
No reference cited.

Chapter 13: Satan and the Jinns – The Differences
No reference cited.

Chapter 14: The Psychological Nature of the Jinns
No reference cited.

Chapter 15: Influences of Satan on the Human Being
1. Sunan Abu Dawood, Volume 3, p. 1390, #4976.
2. Mufti Muhammad Shafi, "Maarif-ul-Quran," (in Urdu), Adarah Al-Maarif, Karachi, Pakistan, 1988, Volume 8, page 853, Explanation of Surah An-Naas. Reported by Anas[RA] in Sahih Bukhari and Sahih Muslim.
3. Mufti Muhammad Shafi, "Maarif-ul-Quran," (in Urdu), Adarah Al-Maarif, Karachi, Pakistan, 1988, Volume 8, page 852, Explanation of Surah An-Naas. Reported by Abu Yaali through Anas[RA] in Tafseer Mazhari.
4. Al-Qardawi, Yusuf, "The Lawful and the Prohibited in Islam (Al-Halal wal Haram fil Islam)," Americaan Trust Publiations, p. 150.

Chapter 16: Summary
No reference cited.

Chapter 17: The Origin of the Angels
a. Al-Hilali, M. T. and Khan, M. M., "Interpretation of the Meaning of The Noble Quran in the English Language," Maktba Dar-us-Salam, Riyadh, Saudi Arabia, 1985.
2. Fakhry, M., "An Interpretation of the Qur'an," New York University Press, Washington Square, New York, 2002.
3. Shafi, M., "Maarif-ul-Quran," Idarah Al-Maarif, Karachi, Pakistan, 1987, Vol. 6 (Urdu), p.21.
4. Greene, B., "The Fabric of Cosmos," Vintage Books, New York, 2005, Cahpter 3.
5. Serway, R. A. and Faughn, J. S., "College Physics," Fifth Edition, Saunders College Publishing, 1999, p. 863.
6. Greene, B., "The Elegant Universe," Vintage Books, New York, 2003, p. 52.
7. Greene, B., "The Elegant Universe," Vintage Books, New York, 2003, p. 150.
8. Greene, B., "The Elegant Universe," Vintage Books, New York, 2003, p. 96.
9. Greene, B., "The Elegant Universe," Vintage Books, New York, 2003, pp. 96.
10. Greene, B., "The Elegant Universe," Vintage Books, New York,

2003, p. 24.
11. Greene, B., "The Elegant Universe," Vintage Books, New York, 2003, pp. 10-13.
12. Maududi, S. A. A., "The Meaning of the Quran," Explanatory Note No. 3 of Surah Fatir (35).
13. Shafi, M., "Ma'arif-ul-Quran," Idarah Al-Maarif, Karachi, Pakistan, 1988, (Urdu), Volume 7, page 317.
14. Maududi, S. A. A., "The Meaning of the Quran," Explanatory Note No. 3 of Surah Fatir (35).
15. Maududi, S. A. A., "The Meaning of the Quran," Explanatory Note No. 3 of Surah Fatir (35).
16. Ali, A. Y., "The Meaning of the Holy Quran," Amana Publications, Beltsville, Maryland, 1989, Explanatory Note No. 5092.
17. Ali, A. Y., "The Meaning of the Holy Quran," Amana Publications, Beltsville, Maryland, 1989, Explanatory Note No. 3871.
18. Maududi, S. A. A., "The Meaning of the Quran," Explanatory Note No. 2 of Surah Fatir (35).
19. Greene, B., "The Elegant Universe," Vintage Books, New York, 2003, p. 94.
20. Serway, R. A. and Faughn, J. S., "College Physics," Fifth Edition, Saunders College Publishing, 1999, pp. 709-711.
21. Greene, B., "The Elegant Universe," Vintage Books, New York, 2003, p. 349.

Chapter 18: The Physical Characteristics of the Angels
a. Dean, J. A. (Ed.), "Lange's Handbook of Chemistry," McGraw-Hill Book Company, 1985, p. 8-38.
2. Ali, A. Y., "The Meaning of the Holy Quran," Amana Publications, Beltsville, Maryland, 1989, Explanatory Note No. 4031.
3. Dean, J. A. (Ed.), "Lange's Handbook of Chemistry," McGraw-Hill Book Company, 1985, p. 8-38.
4. Greene, B., "The Elegant Universe," Vintage Books, New York, 2003, p. 24.
5. Maududi, S. A. A., "The Meaning of the Quran," Explanatory Note No. 3 of Surah Fatir (35).
6. Maududi, S. A. A., "The Meaning of the Quran," Explanatory Note No. 3 of Surah Fatir (35).
7. Ali, A. Y., "The Meaning of the Holy Quran," Amana Publications, Beltsville, Maryland, 1989, Explanatory Note No. 5092.
8. Dean, J. A. (Ed.), "Lange's Handbook of Chemistry," McGraw-Hill Book Company, 1985, p. 8-38.
9. Dean, J. A. (Ed.), "Lange's Handbook of Chemistry," McGraw-Hill Book Company, 1985, p. 8-38.

10. Serway, R. A. and Faughn, J. S., "College Physics," Fifth Edition, Saunders College Publishing, 1999, p. 136

Chapter 19: The Biological Characteristics of the Angels
a. Greene, B., "The Elegant Universe," Vintage Books, New York, 2003, pp. 346-356.
2. Adams, F. and Laughln, G., "The Five Ages of the Universe," Simon and Schuster, 1999, p. 34.
3. Ali, A. Y., "The Meaning of the Holy Quran," Amana Publications, Beltsville, Maryland, 1989, Explanatory Note No. 4343.
4. Maududi, S. A. A., "The Meaning of the Quran," Explanatory Note No. 47 of Surah Al-Anaam (6) and Explanatory Note No. 57 of Surah Ibraheem (14).
5. Shafi, Mufti Muhammad, "Maarif-ul-Quran, Idarah Al-Maarif, Karachi, Pakistan, 1988, (Urdu), Explanation of Verse No. 87 of Surah An-Naml (27) (p. 607 of Volume 6) and Verse No. 68 of Surah Az-Zuamr (39) (p.577 of Volume 7).
6. Greene, B., "The Elegant Universe," Vintage Books, New York, 2003, pp. 41- 42.
7. Greene, B., "The Elegant Universe," Vintage Books, New York, 2003, p. 51.
8. Greene, B., "The Elegant Universe," Vintage Books, New York, 2003, p. 82.
9. Greene, B., "The Elegant Universe," Vintage Books, New York, 2003, p. 346.
10. Greene, B., "The Elegant Universe," Vintage Books, New York, 2003, p. 82.
11. Greene, B., "The Elegant Universe," Vintage Books, New York, 2003, pp. 234-235.
12. Greene, B., "The Elegant Universe," Vintage Books, New York, 2003, pp. 10-13.
13. Ali, A. Y., "The Meaning of the Holy Quran," Amana Publications, Beltsville, Maryland, 1989, Explanatory Note No. 5006.
14. Mufti Muhammad Shafi, "Maarif-ul-Quran," Adarah Al-Maarif, Karachi, Pakistan, 1988, Volume 8, page 852-3," Explanation of Surah An-Naas. Reported Abu Yaali through Anas[RA] in Tafseer Mazhari.
15. Bukhari, Volume 4, No. 429.

Chapter 20: The Intellectual Ability of the Angels
a. Hooper, J. and Tersel, D., "The Three-Pound Universe," G. P. Putnam's Sons, New Yoirk, 1986, pp. 53-59.
2. Mufti Muhammad Shafi, "Maarif-ul-Quran," Adarah Al-Maarif,

Karachi, Pakistan, 1988, Volume 8, page 852-3," Explanation of Surah An-Naas. Reported Abu Yaali through Anas[RA] in Tafseer Mazhari.
3. Maududi, A. A., "The Meaning of the Quran, Islamic Publications Ltd., Lahore, Pakistan, 1980, Explanatory Note No. 43 of Surah Al-Baqarah.

Chapter 21: The Spiritual Nature of the Angels

Chapter 22: The Functions of the Angels
a. Ali, A. Y., "The Meaning of the Holy Quran," Amana Publications, Beltsville, Maryland, 1989, Explanatory Note No. 4031.
2. Sabiq, As-Sayyid, "Fiqh us-Sunnah – Supererogatory Pryaer," Vol. IV, 1992, American Trust Publications, Indianapolis, IN, Chapter 5, p.92.
3. Sabiq, As-Sayyid, "Fiqh us-Sunnah – Supererogatory Pryaer," Vol. IV, 1992, American Trust Publications, Indianapolis, IN, Chapter 5, p.92.
4. Sabiq, As-Sayyid, "Fiqh us-Sunnah – Supererogatory Pryaer," Vol. IV, 1992, American Trust Publications, Indianapolis, IN, Chapter 5, p.92.

Chapter 23: The Famous Angels
a. Al-Hilali, M. T. and Khan, M. M., "Interpretation of the Meaning of The Noble Quran in the English Language," Maktba Dar-us-Salam, Riyadh, Saudi Arabia, 1985.
2. Fakhry, M., "An Interpretation of the Qur'an," New York University Press, Washington Square, New York, 2002.
3. Shafi, M., "Maarif-ul-Quran," Idarah Al-Maarif, Karachi, Pakistan, 1987, Vol. 6 (Urdu), p.21.
4. Maududi, S. A. A., "The Meaning of the Quran," Explanatory Note No. 3 of Surah Fatir (35).
5. Maududi, S. A. A., "The Meaning of the Quran," Explanatory Note No. 3 of Surah Fatir (35).
6. Islahi, M. Y., "Asan Fiqh," Vol. 1 (Urdu), Pan Islamic Publicaitons, Lahore, 1976, p. 74.
7. Encyclopaedia Britannica Micropaedia Volume I, 1977, p. 486.
8. Karim, Fazl, "Al-Hadis – An English Translation & Commentary of Mishkat-ul-Masabih," Book IV, Islamic Book Service, New Delhi, India, 1989, p. 93.
9. Shafi, M., "Maarif-ul-Quran," Idarah Al-Maarif, Karachi, Pakistan, 1987, Vol. 7 (Urdu), pp. 67-68.
10. Maududi, S. A. A., "The Meaning of the Quran," Explanatory Note No. 104-a of Surah Al-Baqarah (2).

11. Sabiq, As-Sayyid, "Fiqh us-Sunnah – Supererogatory Pryaer," Vol. IV, 1992, American Trust Publications, Indianapolis, IN, Chapter 5, p.90.
12. Sabiq, As-Sayyid, "Fiqh us-Sunnah – Supererogatory Pryaer," Vol. IV, 1992, American Trust Publications, Indianapolis, IN, Chapter 5, p.90.
13. Sabiq, As-Sayyid, "Fiqh us-Sunnah – Supererogatory Pryaer," Vol. IV, 1992, American Trust Publications, Indianapolis, IN, Chapter 5, p.92.
14. Sabiq, As-Sayyid, "Fiqh us-Sunnah – Supererogatory Pryaer," Vol. IV, 1992, American Trust Publications, Indianapolis, IN, Chapter 5, p.92.
15. Sabiq, As-Sayyid, "Fiqh us-Sunnah – Supererogatory Pryaer," Vol. IV, 1992, American Trust Publications, Indianapolis, IN, Chapter 5, p.92.
16. Sabiq, As-Sayyid, "Fiqh us-Sunnah – Supererogatory Pryaer," Vol. II, 1992, American Trust Publications, Indianapolis, IN, Chapter 1, p.6.

Chapter 24: The Angels and the Humans
a. Shafi, M., "Maarif-ul-Quran," Adarah Al-Maarif, Karachi, Pakistan, 1988, Volume 8 (Urdu), page 853, Explanatin of Surah An-Naas, Reported by Abu Yaali through Anas in Tafseer Mazhari.
2. Shafi, M., "Maarif-ul-Quran," Adarah Al-Maarif, Karachi, Pakistan, 1988, Volume 8 (Urdu), page 853, Explanatin of Surah An-Naas, Reported by Abu Yaali through Anas in Tafseer Mazhari.
3. The Random House Childrens Encyclopedia, Random House, New York, 1991, p. 454.
4. The Random House Childrens Encyclopedia, Random House, New York, 1991, p. 454.

Chapter 25: Summary

Chapter 26: The Demons
1. The New Encyclopedia Britannica, Encyclopedia Britannica, Inc., 1977, Volume 1, pp. 871-876.
2. Matthew 9:32-33, Luke 11:14.
3. Mark 1: 23-26, Luke 4:33-35.
4. Mark 5:1-15, Matthew 8:28-33, Luke 8:26-36.
5. Mark 9:14-28, Matthew 17:14-21, Luke 9:37-43.
6. Mufti Muhammad Shafi, "Maarif-ul-Quran," Adarah Al-Maarif, Karachi, Pakistan, 1988, Volume 8, page 852-3," Explanation of Surah An-Naas. Reported Abu Yaali through Anas[RA] in Tafseer Mazhari.
7. Snyder, C. H., "The Extraordinary Chemistry of Ordinary Things,"

John Wiley and Sons, Inc., 2nd Edition, 1995, pp. 307-311
8. Kunz, J. R. M., "The American Medical Association Family Medical Guide," Random House, New York, 1982, p. 656.
9. Sunan Abu Dawood, Volume 3, p. 1390, #4976.
10. Mufti Muhammad Shafi, "Maarif-ul-Quran," (in Urdu), Adarah Al-Maarif, Karachi, Pakistan, 1988, Volume 8, page 853, Explanation of Surah An-Naas. Reported by Anas^{RA} in Sahih Bukhari and Sahih Muslim.

Chapter 27: The Angels, the Demons, Satan, the Jinns, and the Humans
No reference cited.

Appendix A: Satan and Adam^{AS} – The Sequence of the Quranic Events
No reference cited.

Appendix B: Electromagnetic Waves
a. Ganic, E. N. and Hicks, T. G., "The McGraw-Hill Handbook of Essential Engineering Information and Data," McGraw-Hill, Inc., New York, 1991, p. 11.12.
2. Greene, B., "The Elegant Universe," Vintage Books, 2003, p. 89.
3. Ganic, E. N. and Hicks, T. G., "The McGraw-Hill Handbook of Essential Engineering Information and Data," McGraw-Hill, Inc., New York, 1991, p. 11.15.
4. Serway, R. A. and Faughn, J. S., "College Physics," Fifth Edition, Saunders College Publishing, 1999, pp. 709-711.
5. The New Encyclopaedia Britannica - Macropaedia Knowledge in Depth, Encyclopaedia Britanica Inc., 15th Ed., 1977, Volume 5, p. 200.

Appendix C: The Origin of the Angels – the Other Possibility
a. Greene, B., "The Elegant Universe," Vintage Books, New York, 2003, p. 11.
2. Greene, B., "The Elegant Universe," Vintage Books, New York, 2003, pp. 10-13.
3. Greene, B., "The Elegant Universe," Vintage Books, New York, 2003, p. 11.
4. Adams, F. and Laughlin, G., "The Five Ages of the Universe," Simon and Schuster, New York, 1999, p. xviii.
5. Adams, F. and Laughlin, G., "The Five Ages of the Universe," Simon and Schuster, New York, 1999, pp. xvii-xviii.
6. Greene, B., "The Elegant Universe," Vintage Books, New York, 2003, pp. 10-13.

7. Adams, F. and Laughlin, G., "The Five Ages of the Universe," Simon and Schuster, New York, 1999, pp. xviii-xix.
8. Ali, A. Y., "The Meaning of the Holy Quran," Amana Publications, Beltsville, Maryland, 1989, Explanatory Note No. 3871.
9. Maududi, S. A. A., "The Meaning of the Quran," Explanatory Note No. 2 of Surah Fatir (35).
10. Greene, B., "The Fabric of Cosmos," Vintage Books, New York, 2003, pp. 254-256.
11. Greene, B., "The Elegant Universe," Vintage Books, New York, 2003, pp. 123-124.
12. Greene, B., "The Fabric of Cosmos," Vintage Books, New York, 2003, pp. 254-256.
13. Greene, B., "The Elegant Universe," Vintage Books, New York, 2003, pp. 123-124.